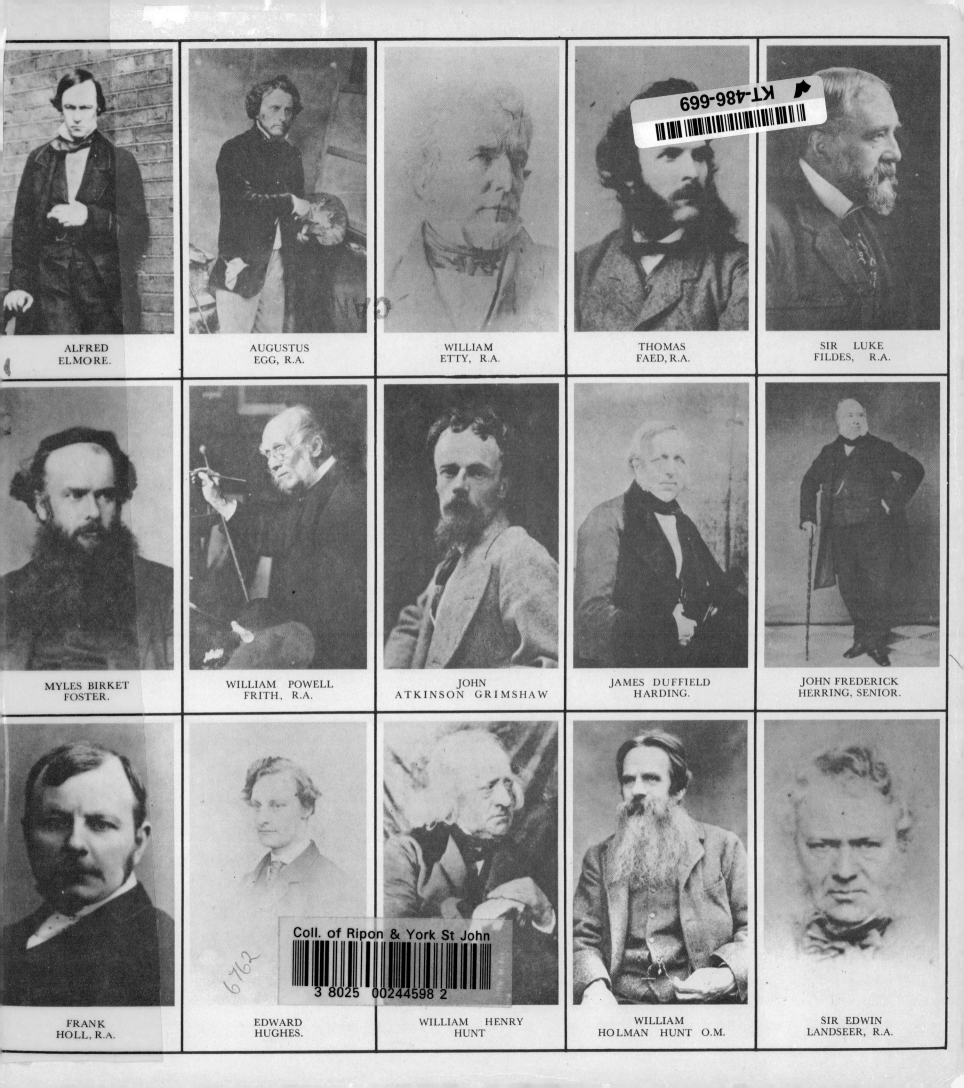

ALFRED
ELMORE.

AUGUSTUS
EGG, R.A.

WILLIAM
ETTY, R.A.

THOMAS
FAED, R.A.

SIR LUKE
FILDES, R.A.

MYLES BIRKET
FOSTER.

WILLIAM POWELL
FRITH, R.A.

JOHN
ATKINSON GRIMSHAW

JAMES DUFFIELD
HARDING.

JOHN FREDERICK
HERRING, SENIOR.

FRANK
HOLL, R.A.

EDWARD
HUGHES.

WILLIAM HENRY
HUNT

WILLIAM
HOLMAN HUNT O.M.

SIR EDWIN
LANDSEER, R.A.

Victorian Painters

VICTORIAN PAINTERS

JEREMY MAAS

AN ARTABRAS BOOK

HARRISON HOUSE • PUBLISHERS • NEW YORK

Printed in Spain.

Library of Congress Cataloging in Publication Data

Maas, Jeremy
    Victorian painters.
    Reprint. Previously published: New York : Putnam,
1969.
    Bibliography: p.
    Includes index.
    1. Painting, British.   2. Painting, Victorian—Great
Britain.   I. Title.
ND467.M26   1984   759.2   84-6240
ISBN 0-517-67131-X

h g f e d c b a

CONTENTS

NOTE ON THE CAPTIONS. All pictures are painted in oils and on canvas unless otherwise stated.

FOREWORD

This survey is an attempt to describe the character and trace the development of Victorian painting. In it I have tried to pursue a hazardous course between the general and the particular, and, in doing so, the dangers inherent in both have become increasingly apparent to me. Inevitably I came to see the truth of Carlyle's belief that 'history is the essence of innumerable biographies'.

I have tried to make this account as comprehensive as possible, but I must ask the indulgence of those who own paintings of merit by artists who are not mentioned in it. In assessing the merits of the painters who are mentioned, I have attempted a synthesis of current attitudes, seasoned with personal bias and with the estimates of the painter's contemporaries. I have quoted no less freely from critics like Thackeray and Henry James than from Ruskin, and have consulted a large number of sources to the authors of which I am greatly indebted. The bibliography also includes a few works enjoying scholarly approval, which I have only briefly, perhaps too briefly, consulted.

I am indebted to numerous galleries and museums, to their trustees, corporate bodies and private owners, whose generosity and patience have been tried to the limit. I hope that they will accept the acknowledgments in the captions to the plates as sufficient token of my gratitude. I would also like to thank all those, too many to enumerate, who have in any way contributed to this book: they include many people whose daily business has been interrupted by endless enquiries over the telephone.

I would particularly like to thank Mr Henry Ford for his constant vigilance over the typescript as it appeared and for his many helpful suggestions. My thanks are also due to Mr Nicolas Barker and Mr John Dent, and I am also very grateful to Miss Sarah Alexander who typed the script. Mr Dennis Farr of the Department of Fine Art at Glasgow University, Mr Edward Malins, Mr Eric Adams, Mr David Fuller of Arthur Ackermann & Son Ltd, Mr E. H. H. Archibald of the National Maritime Museum, Dr Jerrold N. Moore of Yale University, Mr Peyton Skipwith of the Fine Art Society Ltd, and Mr John Rickett of Sotheby & Co., all read sections of the book in typescript and made valuable suggestions, for which I offer my most sincere thanks. I would also like to record my gratitude to Mr Dudley Snelgrove of The Paul Mellon Foundation, Mrs Pat Hodgson, Mr Richard Ormond of the National Portrait Gallery, Mr John Hayes of the London Museum, Mr J. L. Howgego of the Guildhall Art Gallery, Mr Wilfrid Blunt, the Curator of The Watts Gallery, Mrs Virginia Surtees, Mr Robin de Beaumont, Miss Mary Lutyens, Mrs Charlotte Frank (whose patience must have been sorely tried during the two sessions of photography on *The Plains of Heaven*), Mr Charles Handley-Read, Mrs Anna Allen of the Tate Gallery, Miss Sophia Ryde, Miss Diana Holman Hunt, Mr Sidney Hutchison, Librarian of the Royal Academy, and his assistant, Miss Constance-Anne Parker, Mr James S. Dearden of The Ruskin Galleries at Bembridge School, Mr Edmund Brudenell, Mr Charles Jerdein, Mr N. R. Omell, Lady Rosalie Mander, Miss Mary Bennett of the Walker Art Gallery, Liverpool and Mr Alec Cotman of the Castle Museum, Norwich.

Mr Guy Phillips kindly allowed me to read and quote from his unpublished monograph on his grandfather, Atkinson Grimshaw, and Westminster City Libraries have given me permission to quote from a letter in their possession. My special thanks are due to Messrs Rodney Todd-White, who photographed many of the pictures, including the majority of the colour plates. Lastly, I would like to thank those friends and relations who have had to tolerate (I would like to think that this is the right word) my unaccustomed desire for seclusion during the writing of this book; particularly my wife, whose help and forbearance I have greatly appreciated.

J. S. M.

I

SURVEY

komer, Alma-Tadema, Tissot, Whistler and Sargent. Writing in 1895 the French critic Robert de la Sizeranne summed it up: 'There is an English school of painting. This is what first strikes a visitor to any International Exhibition of the Fine Arts, in whatever country it might be held.' In the galleries of other countries, he said, 'you might imagine yourself to be still in France', so dependent were their artists on Paris. Not so the English: 'Their painters seem to ignore the Continent. If they have heard of it they have borrowed nothing from it. They have thrown no bridge across the Channel.' (However, he later took into account the aspirations of the New English Art Club, formed in 1885, whose members painted 'a mass of mediocre pictures . . . more or less like our own'.) He continues: 'Fifty years ago, when we were adopting a broader manner wherein drawing played a smaller part and details were sacrificed to the whole, our neighbours were reversing the process, and entering on the minutiae of the Primitives. At the present time, when the open-air school has lighted up most of our canvases, they remain boldly faithful to their startling colouring, to their laboured and complicated modelling. The assaults of realism and of impressionism are broken on their aestheticism, like the squadrons of Ney

During Queen Victoria's reign, the history of painting in England becomes an infinitely complex skein of extraordinary richness and variety. There were contradictions, movements and counter-movements; endless and labyrinthine courses were explored, false gods pursued; and a quantity of abysmal work was produced. It was nevertheless a great age for English painting. If the period produced few artists of world stature, this was balanced by the cumulative effect of the rich diversity of high talent, occasionally bordering on greatness. If the parts are sometimes leaden, the whole is a bright golden glow. This is nowhere more obvious than in the case of the Pre-Raphaelites: seen in isolation, the work of individual artists often appears maladroit, but grouped together their brilliance is manifest, and their very failings are forgiven in the way that one condones the eccentricities of genius.

For all its weaknesses, the English School had a prevailing strength and vigour during the Victorian age that was internationally recognised, and it even served as a refuge to many foreign artists, like Her-

on the squares of Wellington. There are German, Hungarian, Belgian, Spanish, Scandinavian painters, but there is an English School of painting.' This is an apt summary of the individuality of English art in the Victorian age, although, at the time that it was written, internationalism was encroaching on indigenous attitudes.

If English painting of the period tended to be insular, it was sometimes surprisingly anticipatory. Notable visiting French artists, like Géricault, were often aware of this. He greatly admired the animal paintings of Ward and Landseer; and Delacroix was deeply affected by his first contact with the paintings of Constable. Turner anticipated both Impressionism and Abstract Expressionism, and French artists—like Renoir and Monet in 1870—were discovering his work for the first time. William Henry Hunt, by hatching broken colours together, anticipated the pointillism of the neo-impressionists; similarly G. F. Watts discovered in mid-century the technique of placing strokes of broken colour together. The quest for pictorial exactitude led the Pre-Raphaelites to paint outdoors directly from nature, thus anticipating the *pleinairisme* of the French impressionists by well over a decade.

JOSEPH MALLORD WILLIAM TURNER, R.A. *Interior at Petworth.* $35\frac{3}{4} \times 47\frac{3}{4}$ inches. Tate Gallery, London.

Painted in about 1837. Turner had been a regular visitor to Petworth for about seven years prior to painting this picture. His friend and patron Lord Egremont died in November 1837.

ALFRED STEVENS. *An Artist in his Studio.* 23⅝ × 18¾ inches. Tate Gallery, London.

Probably painted in 1840-2 at Rome towards the end of the artist's stay in Italy.

Whilst there is a vast amount of documentation covering Victorian painting, areas of doubt still remain and biographical uncertainties abound. Artists known to have flourished appear to have left a meagre legacy of paintings; paintings of great quality by artists barely heard of are still surfacing after a long period of submersion. There are scores of painters whose fame rests on just one or two paintings, like W. S. Burton with *The Wounded Cavalier* and Henry Wallis with *The Death of Chatterton*, although the former exhibited at the Royal Academy and British Institution for thirty years and the latter painted a number of pictures in the 'fifties, earning the approbation of Ruskin. In a survey of this period one is often compelled 'to row out', as Lytton Strachey said, 'over the great ocean of material and lower down into it, here and there, a little bucket, which will bring up to the light of day some characteristic specimen, from those far depths, to be examined with a careful curiosity'.

But in the ebb and flow of contradictory currents, certain beacons light the way. The existence of the Royal Academy, founded in 1768, acted simultaneously as a focus for the artistic endeavours of British painters and as an institution for certain movements to react against. Either way it constituted an energising force. The first self-conscious art movement occurred during the first year of the Queen's reign, but never actually went anywhere. It was really a kind of rebellion against authority, the authority vested in the Royal Academy. This was the formation of 'The Clique': a group of painters comprising Augustus Egg, Richard Dadd, John Phillip, H. N. O'Neil and W. P. Frith. Their aim was to revitalize what to them was the stuffy traditionalism of the Royal Academy. They were all extremely young: it was essentially a revolt of youth against age, but it also amounted to a worthy effort to *paint* better. The individuals in the group had divergent aims, which reflected the diversity of British painting as a whole. Dadd wanted to paint works of imagination; Egg, illustrations of celebrated literary works; Phillip, incidents in the lives of the famous; O'Neil, pictures which appealed to the feelings and Frith, scenes of ordinary life. Later in the century another group formed itself, with P. H. Calderon at its head, into the 'St. John's Wood Clique', which included W. F. Yeames, H. S. Marks, G. A. Storey and others, but this second group seemed to lack any clearly defined directional impulse.

Then there was the growth of private patronage, personified by men like Robert Vernon, who had accumulated a fortune by supplying horses to the army during the Napoleonic Wars. By commissioning directly from the artist he managed to assemble a magnificent collection, which is now in the Tate Gallery; similarly John Sheepshanks, the scion of an

industrial Yorkshire family, formed a collection which is now at the Victoria and Albert Museum. The Queen and Prince Albert bought a number of contemporary

WILLIAM HUGGINS. *The Stoic.* 24 × 29 inches. Private collection, Great Britain.

Inscribed on the reverse: 'one who is free from passion unmoved by joy or grief indifferent to pain or pleasure'.

ALFRED STEVENS. *King Alfred and his Mother.* Panel. 13½ × 13½ inches. Tate Gallery, London. Painted in about 1848.

GEORGE FREDERICK WATTS,
O.M., R.A. *Lady Margaret Beaumont
and her Daughter.* 76 × 45½ inches.

The Rt Hon. Viscount Allendale.
Painted in 1862. Lady Margaret
Beaumont (d. 1888) married the

1st Baron Allendale in 1856. Her
daughter, Magaret Harriet, later
became Lady Poltimore.

works, and did much in the way of patronage, including the granting of honours. By conferring knighthoods, baronetcies and one peerage (Leighton) on her painter subjects, the Queen raised the prestige of painting.

And never, before or since, had the prestige of English artists been so high. The letters of the period frequently refer to art and artists; and the earnings of painters, who dressed like gentlemen and often moved with ease on the hunting field or in the drawing-rooms of High Society, were correspondingly high, often through the sale of engraving rights. Millais, at the height of his fame, reputedly earned between £20,000 and £40,000 a year and is believed to have sold his *The North-West Passage* for 4,700 guineas. Frith was commissioned to record the Prince of Wales's wedding for a fee of 3,000 guineas, and reputedly collected another 5,000 guineas from the sale of the copyright to the dealer, Flatow. Holman Hunt, who was advised by Dickens on what to charge for his work, probably made the highest sum ever paid to a living British artist for an easel picture in selling the second replica of *The Light of the World* to Charles Booth for 12,000 guineas. Booth presented it to St. Paul's Cathedral, the resting place of Landseer, Turner, Leighton, Millais, Alma-Tadema, Poynter and Holman Hunt. Hunt left £163,000 with painting as his sole means of support since the age of sixteen, and with negligible help from studio assistants. At least three Victorian painters left over £200,000: they were Landseer, Linnell and John Gilbert, most of whose income was from illustration.

It was truly a prodigious age. It was the age of the polymathic artist: everyone seemed to be doing everything at once. 'It was a world', wrote G. K. Chesterton, 'in which painters were trying to be novelists, and novelists trying to be historians, and musicians doing the work of schoolmasters, and sculptors doing the work of curates'; and creative talent was dissipated in diversity. William Dyce was the archetypal *homo universalis:* science, music, church ritual, teaching and other pursuits fragmented his creative impulse. Leighton, Poynter, Stevens, Redgrave and W. B. Richmond, to name only a few, spread their energies over a wide field of activities, thus restricting their output of painting. Again and again one encounters an artist of promise whose talents were unseasonably employed on academic or other official duties.

State patronage was a mixed blessing. The status of art, particularly applied art, was enhanced by the two great International Exhibitions of 1851 and 1862. On the other hand the decoration of the rebuilt Houses of Parliament (1841–63) was a fiasco, although it had at least one beneficial result, in that it dealt the death blow to historical painting, a *genre* for which English painters were in every way unsuited; and the failure of Benjamin Robert Haydon, its arch-priest, to secure a prize contributed to his depression and eventual suicide in 1846, and ensured the total demise of historical painting as a force in English art.

The foundation of Morris and Company (1861), of the Art Workers Guild (1884) and the New English Art Club (1885), all of which had their roots in rebellion, are all milestones in the growth and development of artistic attitudes and public taste. The most vigorous seeds of rebellion were contained in what Henry James called 'the first fresh fruits of the Pre-Raphaelite efflorescence'. The forming of the Pre-Raphaelite Brotherhood in 1848, a revolutionary year throughout Europe, gave rise from the start to detonations which shook the very foundations of the artistic Establishment and echoed down the years to the death of the Queen in 1901, and even beyond.

Pre-Raphaelitism has been too often dismissed as a regrettable aberration in the English psyche, a brief period of madness, only redeemed by the tardy introduction of Impressionism by the New English Art Club. In fact, the influence of Pre-Raphaelitism, although its course is strewn with individual tragedies, was greatly beneficial. Apart from the qualified

SIR FRANK DICKSEE, P.R.A. *Harmony.* (detail) Arched top. 62 × 37 inches. Signed and dated 1877. Tate Gallery, London.

Exhibited at the Royal Academy in 1877. This picture achieved immense popularity at the time, and was bought by the Chantrey Bequest. At the Academy exhibition it was hung in the place of honour opposite Millais's *Yeoman of the Guard.*

partisan, John Ruskin, many writers of the period, some not otherwise known for being sympathetic to the movement, admitted as much. P. G. Hamerton, writing in 1889, noted that Pre-Raphaelitism was 'a strong and beneficial reaction from indolent synthesis to laborious analysis, and from mental inactivity to new thought and emotion'. Another writer, G. H. Shepherd, echoed these sentiments when he wrote that 'The influence of the Pre-Raphaelite School upon the art of the last quarter of a century has been undoubtedly

JOHN RUSKIN. *Church and Vista on the Bay of Naples.* Water-colour. 15⅝ × 11¼ inches. Vassar College Art Gallery, Poughkeepsie.

Ruskin described the scene in his diary on 1st March 1841, 'I never saw a finer thing . . . a little chapel pitched half way up, with a bold arch of natural rock, and another of a ruined bridge; and the tower of a convent on the walls bright against the uppermost blue sky, formed a scene almost too theatrical to be quite right'.

beneficial. It has inculcated the direct study of Nature, paying little regard to conventional rules borrowed from the antique; and, although it has erred by undue contempt for principles of composition based upon centuries of experience, it has effected a reformation of great good'. Even the reliable Redgrave brothers, whose 'A Century of Painters' appeared in 1866, agreed that 'on the whole we feel that the future prospects of art will be improved rather than injured by the outbreak of what has been idly called the "new heresy".'

The Pre-Raphaelites made artists *see* and paint what they saw with unprecedented skill; and they made a whole generation of designers and practitioners of the applied arts see anew and invest their work with an entirely new range of symbolism. As Walter Crane wrote in the 'Fortnightly Review' in December 1892, 'by their resolute and enthusiastic return to the direct symbolism, frank naturalism, and poetic or romantic sentiment of mediaeval art, with the power of modern analysis superadded, and the more profound and intellectual study of both nature and art which the severity of their practice demanded, and last, but not least, their intense love of detail, turned the attention to other branches of design than painting'. Moreover, the works of Rossetti and, in particular, Burne-Jones, by virtue of their complete distinction from the naturalistic school, had a profound effect on the formative years of such twentieth century figures as Picasso and Kandinsky, just as they appealed to the French symbolists before the turn of the century.

As a result of his advocacy, the Pre-Raphaelite movement finally established the aesthetic despotism of the critic John Ruskin, whose generally beneficial but sometimes disastrous 'reign of terror' only ended with the calamitous collision with Whistler in a libel action nearly thirty years later. Ruskin's influence over the course of mid-Victorian painting was enormous. In the 'fifties painters would doggedly paint according to his precepts: he had only to wonder why no-one ever painted apple-trees in blossom for the Academy walls a year later to be covered with orchards full of apple-trees in blossom. Ruskin also acted as a link between Pre-Raphaelitism and the applied arts. 'It is he', as Mr Denys Sutton has suggested, 'who provides a valid explanation of the love of "finish" which meant so much to the typical Victorian painter: he reminds us that this desire to produce a well turned out product was the counterpart to the solidity of English manu-factured goods and furniture.' Ruskin's writings on the Old Masters, architecture and the structure of Society, and his vindication of Turner, were of incalculable value to the formation of Victorian taste and *mores*.

The taste of the picture-buying public was an important element, influencing as it did the course of Victorian painting. William Makepeace Thackeray, an exuberant but very sensible art critic in the 'forties, was appalled at the state of public taste at the time. Writing in 'Fraser's Magazine' in 1840 he jocularly stated his intention of drawing up 'Proposals for the General Improvement of Public Taste', although this intention was not fulfilled. While he praised faintly, he

GEORGE FREDERICK WATTS, O.M., R.A. *Ariadne in Naxos.* $29\frac{1}{2} \times 37$ inches. Guildhall Art Gallery, London.

Painted between 1867 and 1875 Watts considered that '*Ariadne* is perhaps the most complete picture I have painted'. There is an almost identical version at Liverpool, and three other versions which differ in details. *See p. 29.*

GEORGE FREDERICK WATTS,
O.M., R.A. *The Sower of the Systems*.
26 × 21 inches. Watts Gallery,
Compton.
    Painted in 1902. Watts wrote:
'This subject was suggested by the
reflection upon the ceiling from a
night light. In this the painter's
imagination saw the veiled figure,
projected as it were, through space
– the track marked by planets, suns
and stars cast from hand and foot.'
A larger and more developed version
was exhibited at Newcastle in 1905.

SIR WILLIAM QUILLER OR-
CHARDSON, R.A. *Her First Dance.*
40×54½ inches. Signed and dated
1884. Tate Gallery, London.
   The picture was bought by Sir
Henry Tate in the year it was
painted.

JOSEPH CRAWHALL. *Jackdaw.*
Water-colour on linen. 11¼×18
inches. National Gallery of Victoria,
Melbourne.

could never really conceal his mild contempt of the 'ogling beauties' or 'dangerous smiling Delilahs' so fondly painted by Chalon, and other artists of the 'Keepsake' school. And the endless array of pictures with themes from the 'Vicar of Wakefield' and 'Gil Blas' provoked his good-natured wrath. After declaring his refusal ever to mention these two works again, he is nevertheless obliged to comment on yet another *V–c–r of W–kef–ld* later in the review.

The fondness which Wilkie and some of his contemporaries displayed for the Dutch and Flemish anecdotal manner was still reflected in pictures of the period, but admiration for Teutonic paintings was becoming a new factor. The piety and purity of German painting mirrored the growing religious revival. In 1839 'The Art Union' could solemnly declare that the Germans 'are assuredly the great artists of Europe'. The avowed preference of the Prince Consort for Germanic art supported this new enthusiasm. Admiration for the pious and coldly linear paintings of the Nazarene School, a group of German expatriates headed by Peter Cornelius and Friedrich Overbeck, who lived in the early years of the century at a deserted monastery in Italy, contributed to the formation of the Pre-Raphaelite Brotherhood. Not until the late 'fifties and 'sixties was a more Italianate warmth injected into English painting by Rossetti. The neo-classical school, whose principal painters were Leighton, Poynter and Alma-Tadema, heralded the return to Greece and Rome in the early evening light of Victoria's reign. Albert Moore united classical principles with the new cult of Japanese art, which itself reflected an increasing interest in the exotic, culminating in the *fin-de-siècle* fantasies of Beardsley and Conder. Only in the 'eighties did Impressionism find its advocates. Among all these currents and cross-currents were numerous gifted artists who pursued solitary courses, like Etty, Dadd, Lear and Palmer: they enriched the main-stream, as tributaries feed a river. Even the spectre of historical painting still haunted the exhibitions of the early 'nineties, some thirty years after the first appearance of Whistlers' *Nocturnes*.

Meanwhile other influences were at work. It was a great age, above all in the 'sixties, for black and white illustration. At the same time art publishing contributed to public taste and art scholarship. Early magazines, like 'The Keepsake', with its engravings of blushing maidens, helped to establish a prototype of Victorian female beauty. 'The Art Journal', 'The Portfolio' and 'The Magazine of Art' were widely read. The invention of photography had serious implications for artists, and was to affect deeply the techniques of painting. The materials and methods of painting were changed dramatically in the 'fifties. The deleterious use of bitumen, or asphaltum, a tarry compound which never completely dried and was to cause the total ruination of many a picture, was superseded by the new colouring techniques of the Pre-Raphaelites. The mood of change was extended to attitudes towards the choice of media. Much of this was of accidental origin. The experiments of the Pre-Raphaelites, particularly Rossetti, who was always hesitant in his techniques, led to the narrowing of a distinction between oils, water-colours, chalks, body-colours and other media. All were employed, with scant distinction, to express equally valid pictorial statements. In their anticipation of twentieth century painting techniques, these earlier painters were demonstrably modern.

II

HISTORICAL PAINTERS

reminded that he was born in the same year as Bonington. The landscape backgrounds to his animal paintings, which occupied him for the greater part of his life, display a harder Germanic finish, no doubt revealing the influence of Prince Albert. But the landscapes became increasingly incidental to the animals. He is the foremost of a group of artists who painted animals in landscapes, including Thomas Sidney Cooper (1803–1902), who had studied under Verboeckhoven in Brussels. Cooper exhibited assiduously at the Royal Academy, painting up to a short time before his death at the age of ninety-nine. Occasionally, in the mid-fifties, his paintings achieve a Pre-Raphaelite smoothness, but the final reaction to seeing the plethora of cattle scenes is a feeling that cows look better on pasture than on canvas. Cooper

occasionally collaborated with Frederick Richard Lee (1798–1879) who has left an abundant legacy of adequately executed landscapes Neither better nor worse was George Shalders (?1825–1873). Richard Ansdell (1815–1885) was a painter after the pattern of Landseer, often filling his landscapes with four-square portraits of the squirearchy. William Shayer (1788–1879) was another artist as prolific as he was long-lived, exhibiting a total of 426 paintings during his life-time. He belongs to the tradition of Morland and Wheatley, bringing to it a marine flavour. Most of his best landscapes are shore-scenes with fishermen, animals, nets and boats. At his best, he painted very well indeed, but always one senses a fatal conformity. William Witherington (1785–1865) likewise began his career as a direct lineal descendant of the Morland/

DAVID COX, SENIOR. *Rhyl Sands*. 19 × 25 inches. The Rt Hon. Lord Clwyd.

Cox made several replicas of each of his more successful oil paintings, but always contrived to vary the incidents. The large finished, though perhaps least successful of the versions of this picture, is at Birmingham. An earlier version, more closely related to Lord Clwyd's, was probably painted in 1854, and is now at Manchester. *See p. 46.*

53

Wheatley tradition, later changing his style to conform to public demand, and painting like Creswick or Lee. Augustus Wall Callcott (1779–1844) celebrated the Coronation year by being knighted; he died seven years later, one of the first of a line of monumentally Victorian artists. Never more than a pleasing painter, Callcott could turn his hand to almost any kind of landscape to order. Colonel Grant has isolated five main classes in Callcott's work—British Landscape, Flemish views, Italian views, Seascapes and Classical Compositions. In his heyday, lines of carriages waited outside his studio, while distinguished visitors attended his own private view of pictures destined for the Royal Academy on the next day. A revival of interest in Callcott's pictures seems as unlikely now as it was fifty years ago.

William Collins (1788–1847) had a delightfully fresh if limited talent, and had been a friend and disciple of Wilkie. He is often seen at his best in shore-scenes, which, unlike Shayer's, have delicacy and refinement; there is often a group of children in the foreground. Constable, whose landscapes Collins's own sometimes recall, knew him but resented Collins's early success. Writing to Archdeacon Fisher in 1825, he noted that 'Collins has a coast scene with fish as usual, and a landscape like a large cow-turd'. Both in oils and water-colours Collins had a nice, if rather suburban touch. His son, christened Wilkie in tribute to his friend, is remembered as the author of 'The Woman in White'. William Havell (1782–1857) and James Duffield Harding (1797–1863) are better known as water-colourists, although Havell also did oils, often of wooded landscapes somewhat in the manner of early Constable. They are distinctly his own, but the colouring tends to monotony. Harding, praised by Ruskin, was versatile: he produced drawings, water-colours, lithographs and oil-paintings. His oils, although not without merit, today command little attention. The small oils of Thomas Churchyard (1798–1865), executed in or around Woodbridge, Suffolk, have rather more vitality. He had a genuine, if fragile talent but, like F. W. Watts, he had a greater respect for Constable than was healthy for him.

London enjoyed the status of being a centre for all the arts, but had a rival in the city of Norwich, once a city of industry and trade, slumbering peacefully on the River Wensum, seemingly unaware of the Industrial Revolution, which served to increase its isolation. The flat landscape and wide horizons had fired the imagination and talents of East Anglian

JAMES STARK. *Rocks and Trees.* Water-colour. $9 \times 13\frac{1}{4}$ inches. Castle Museum, Norwich.

Opposite page, above:
HENRY PETHER. *The Tower of London by Moonlight.* 22×38 inches. Signed. Ministry of Public Building and Works, London.
  Painted in about 1850-5. *See p. 50.*

Opposite page, below:
FREDERICK WILLIAM WATTS. *A Suffolk Landscape.* 40×54 inches. Arthur Ackermann & Sons Ltd., London. *See p. 48.*

JOHN SELL COTMAN. *From my Father's House at Thorpe.* 27×37 inches. Inscribed and dated 'Jan. 18, 1842'. Castle Museum, Norwich.
  Painted on his return from his last visit to Norfolk in the autumn of 1841.

JOHN MIDDLETON. *Landscape with Pollards.* 20¼ × 24¼ inches. Castle Museum, Norwich.

This picture shows strongly the influence of both Crome and Cotman.

Opposite page, above:
JOHN SELL COTMAN. *Trees on a Hill.* Monochrome wash. 8¾ × 13⅝ inches. Castle Museum, Norwich.

Probably painted on the artist's last visit to Norfolk in the autumn of 1841.

Opposite page, below:
HENRY BRIGHT. *Windmill at Sheringham, Norfolk.* 32 × 52½ inches. Castle Museum, Norwich.

JOHN BERNEY LADBROOKE. *River landscape.* 14 × 21 inches. Signed with monogram and dated 1869. Castle Museum, Norwich.

artists for some fifty years. The first and greatest Norwich School painter, John Crome, had died in 1821, leaving John Sell Cotman (1782–1842) as his most notable successor. Cotman's career had nearly drawn to a close by 1837 and for the last eight years of his life he was drawing-master at King's College in London. During these last years Cotman painted a number of large, strongly coloured water-colours, which often have a highly charged sense of drama. But it is the works of his middle phase which had a profound, if not immediate influence on English landscape painting. His modernity shows in his simplification of natural forms, painted with an apparently cavalier use of colour. A singularly apt tribute to Cotman is contained in Mr John Russell's review of the John Nash exhibition at the Royal Academy in 1967: 'He [Nash] had already learned from Cotman that painters are free to disentangle, simplify and re-organise the facts of Nature. They could leave a lot out, if they felt like it, and they could develop their own habits of emphatic patterning; but those patterns had to be based on a profound understanding of form and not on some sloven's whim.'

The paintings of the Norwich School have a distinct overall personality and this makes attribution a hazardous affair, leaving one with the impression that it makes its greatest impact as a whole rather than through individual artists. However, certain artists like John Middleton (1827–1856), John Berney Ladbrooke (1803–1879), James Stark (1794–1859), Henry Bright (1810–1873), Alfred Stannard (1806–1889), Old Crome's son, John Berney Crome (1794–1842), Cotman's two sons, Miles Edmund (1810–1858) and John Joseph (1814–1878), have sufficient individuality—and indeed far more talent than some of their better known national contemporaries—to set them apart. The greater contribution of the Norwich School is, however, a collective one The view may be local, but the naturalism is universal, and was rarely painted without a high degree of excellence

IV

MARINE PAINTERS

CLARKSON STANFIELD, R.A.
On the Scheldt, near Leiskenshoeck: a
Squally Day. $37\frac{1}{2} \times 50\frac{1}{2}$ inches. Royal
Academy, London.

Exhibited at the Royal Academy
in 1837. Painted in 1837, this was
Clarkson Stanfield's Diploma Work.
He was elected R.A. in 1835.

'From childhood they dabbled in water, they swam like fishes,
their playthings were boats.'—Ralph Waldo Emerson on
the English.

Britain in the nineteenth century was at the height of
her maritime power, and, when Victoria came to the
throne, was the greatest industrial and trading nation
on earth. An island, with no place further than seventy
miles from the sea, the country boasted the world's
mightiest seaport, in the Thames Estuary, from which
the great East Indiamen sailed to the India and China
seas; then there were Newcastle and Bristol, centres of
the coal and tobacco trades respectively, and their
great rival Liverpool, with its trade in cotton and
its command of the Atlantic trade-routes. Despite the
gradual change from sail to steam, the great ships still
presented a romantic appearance, and the skyline of
every port was cross-hatched with masts and rigging,
an alluring prospect to artists of the Island Race. The
painting of water came naturally to landscape
painters, living in a country surrounded by sea and
traversed by innumerable rivers. Discussing the representation of water as a subject for painters in 'The Art
Journal' of January 1863, Professor Ansted noted 'its
infinite mobility; its variety of colour as produced by
reflection and refraction; and its wonderful influence

in forming and changing the features of earth on land and by the sea.'

Many of the English sea painters were essentially landscape painters, although some of them are remembered best for their marine paintings. Incomparably the finest sea painter was Turner. The sea and events connected with it stirred him greatly and inspired him to paint some of his most moving pictures. Often in his marine painting there is a brooding sense of disaster, renewal and change: the sculptor Thomas Woolner describes how Woodington, a fellow sculptor, 'was on a steamboat returning from a trip to Margate when in the midst of a great blazing sunset he saw the old Téméraire drawn by a steam tug (to be broken up at Rotherhithe). The sight was so magnificent that it struck him as being an unusually fine subject for a picture . . . but he was not the only person on board who took professional notice of the splendid sight', for also noticing and making busy little sketches on cards was Turner. The result, *The Fighting Téméraire*, was shown at the Royal Academy in 1839, and was greatly loved by Victorians and by succeeding generations. The terror of storms, tempestuous seas, flapping sails and boatloads of puny humanity inspired some of his finest shipping scenes.

Prodigious events appealed to the great Romantic: when a $14\frac{1}{2}$ foot whale was displayed to the public, Turner, with his usual interest in marine matters, went to see it. This, together with his fondness for reading accounts of whaling in the northern seas, probably inspired a series of whaling pictures painted in 1845–6. Apart from Turner (and Constable and Bonington before the Victorian era), Cotman was the only other painter who treated sea subjects with real genius, although much of his best work had been done before 1837. His ability to achieve grand effects by simplification was something new in English art and was particularly suited to marine painting in watercolours, for rendering broad masses of light and shade.

One of the most distinguished of Victorian sea painters was Clarkson Stanfield (1793–1867). The son of an Irish actor and writer, he was brought up in a seafaring community. Although he showed early promise as a draughtsman, the sea won him, and he entered the Merchant Service in 1808. Four years later he was press-ganged into the Royal Navy, and it was whilst he was on board H.M.S. Namur that he painted scenery for shipboard theatricals. Shortly afterwards he was retired disabled after injuring his foot on an anchor. He took up scene painting in

Dutch Fishing Boats by J. M. W. Turner is reproduced in colour on p. 71.

CLARKSON STANFIELD, R.A. *Shakespeare Cliff.* 23 × 36 inches. Signed and dated 1862. National Maritime Museum, Greenwich.
A life-boat is being made ready to go to a brig in distress.

Edinburgh, and it was here that he formed a lifelong friendship with David Roberts. By 1829 the two artists were working together on large dioramic views, a series of tableaux on a slowly unrolling backcloth. One of Stanfield's included the progress of a ship from its manufacture to its wreck. He soon began to devote more time to easel painting, exhibiting a large number of pictures at the Royal Academy, and becoming a member in 1835. Broken-hearted by the sudden death of his friend Roberts in 1864, Stanfield survived him by less than three years. His pictures show a deep understanding of the sea, but while clouds and water are rendered exactly, they are often betrayed by a theatricality of effect (the canvases are sometimes so cluttered up with driftwood, buoys and other paraphernalia that one wonders how the ships could pursue their courses without extreme peril) and by a lack of real understanding of paint. Clouds and sea never merge, as they do in Turner and Cotman. To Thackeray, Stanfield's style is 'as simple and manly as a seaman's song. One of the most dexterous he is also one of the most careful of painters'. He was too careful for Ruskin who wished him 'less wonderful and

more terrible'. The simple virtues that served him well during his lifetime have not saved him from declining in public estimation. When Stanfield died, Queen Victoria considered Edward William Cooke (1811–1880) to have taken on his mantle. Cooke, who had had no formal training, was taught by his father to paint, draw and engrave. He emerged as a considerable figure on the Victorian scene, both as a painter and as an accomplished scientist, particularly in botany, becoming a Fellow of the Royal Society. In painting he showed more skill than Stanfield, and often worked up his subjects from small sketches done on the spot. Although he had a marvellous eye for detail and feeling for composition, the colours sometimes lack warmth.

Another artist who took up scene painting in his formative years was George Chambers (1803–1840). Born in poverty, the son of a seaman, he went to sea at the age of ten. He was soon delighting his shipmates with his drawings. Although he was never healthy as a boy, his determination and considerable talent, together with the kindly patronage of a Wapping publican, brought him to the notice of the public.

EDWARD WILLIAM COOKE, R.A. *Venice*. 15⅝ × 26¼ inches. Signed and inscribed 'Venezia 1850'. Frank T. Sabin Ltd., London.

From 1827 until his early death he exhibited at the Royal Academy. He was buried, like Bonington, at St. James's Chapel, Pentonville. He was prolific and a more fluent painter than Stanfield, but less fortunate in his rewards. The work of Chambers and Stanfield illustrates the growing naturalism of nineteenth century sea painting, distinguishing it from the mannered tradition of Van de Velde. On the other hand, artists like Turner and David Cox (who was also capable of painting fine sea subjects) were preparing the way for the impressionism of Whistler and Steer. Another element was soon to join these, in the Pre-Raphaelitism of John Brett and Henry Moore. Meanwhile the hackneyed convention of Van de Velde continued to be brilliantly exploited by artists like John Schetky (1778–1874), a Scotsman (despite the name), who exhibited sea paintings at the Royal Academy for nearly seventy years. His paintings are characterised by a lightish palette and rather flat

drawing with a high finish. Schetky was always accurate and sympathetic in his painting, and it seems natural that he should have been employed as Marine Painter by the sea-loving William IV, and later by Queen Victoria. Newcastle produced a sea painter of great, though sometimes uneven, natural talent in James Wilson Carmichael (1800–1868). He lived in his native town until 1845, when, already well-known for his sea pictures, he came to London. Some of the sketches he made in the Baltic during the Crimean war were engraved for 'The Illustrated London News'. Last exhibiting at the Royal Academy in 1859, he retired to Scarborough, where he died.

The tradition of ship portraiture continued to find expression through artists like John Ward (1798–1849), a native of Hull. His work reveals the influence of William Anderson, who died in 1837. In the work of William John Huggins (1781–1845) can be found the ultimate expression of the nineteenth century ship

EDWARD WILLIAM COOKE, R.A. *Beaching a Pink in Heavy Weather at Scheveningen.* 42 × 66 inches. Signed and dated 1855. National Maritime Museum, Greenwich.

Exhibited at the Royal Academy in 1855.

portrait. He was assisted by J. M. Huggins, whose
work is almost undistinguishable. Samuel Walters
(1811–1883) of Liverpool, later assisted by his son
George, painted accurate ship portraits and shipping
scenes; and Joseph Walter (1783–1856), a native of
Bristol, painted in an attractive manner, combining
traditionalism and naturalism. With James Webb
(c.1820–1895) we are brought back to the naturalists:
Webb had a fine feeling for atmosphere and his
pictures are painted with lively freedom.

Two painters who excelled in water-colour contributed substantially to the naturalistic tradition: they
were Edward Duncan (1804–1882) and Antony
Vandyke Copley Fielding (1787–1855). Both enjoyed
a high reputation during their life-time, particularly
the latter; this was due to the championship of Ruskin
who claimed that 'no man has ever given, with the
same flashing freedom, the race of a running tide under
a stiff breeze; nor caught, with the same grace and
precision, the curvature of the breaking wave, arrested
or accelerated by the wind.' Equally at home by the
lake or on the open sea, Copley Fielding did indeed

convey the appearance of water, in a number of brilliantly executed water-colours; many of them are now
sadly faded, owing to his persistent use of indigo.
Duncan, the son-in-law of W. J. Huggins, never achieved
the fame of Copley Fielding during his life-time, but it
is difficult now to escape the conclusion that the quality
of his work was in every way equal to that of Copley
Fielding, and certainly not so uneven. Other excellent
marine water-colourists were Charles Bentley (1806–
1854), William Callow and his brother, John (1822–
1878), Edwin Hayes (1820–1904), another native of
Bristol, William (1803–1867) and John Joy (1806–
1866)—known as 'The Brothers Joy'—whose colla-
boration resulted in an important legacy of water-
colours, Thomas Sewell Robins (d. 1880), who
achieved great popularity, and Thomas Bush Hardy
(1842–1897), a competent but highly repetitive
painter.

The passing of the age of sail was a stimulus to the
historical sea painters, and the romantic history of
naval engagements, voyages of discovery and piracy
supplied the themes. This *genre* produced no great art,

JOHN BRETT, A.R.A. *Echoes of a Far-off Storm.* 42 × 84 inches. Guildhall Art Gallery, London.
Exhibited at the Royal Academy in 1890.

but it contributed to later Victorian iconography. Notable among the practitioners was Oswald Walters Brierly (1817–1894) whose patriotic subjects like *The Retreat of the Spanish Armada* earned him the post of Marine Painter to Queen Victoria. William Lionel Wyllie (1851–1931) was a far more interesting artist.

WILLIAM JOHN HUGGINS. *The Asia East Indiaman in the China Seas.* 32 × 50 inches. Signed and dated 1836. National Maritime Museum, Greenwich.

JAMES SMETHAM. *Seagulls.*
Panel. 4×12 inches. Mrs Virginia
Surtees.

WILLIAM LIONEL WYLLIE,
R.A. *Storm and Sunshine, a Battle with
the Elements.* 42×65 inches. Signed
and dated 1885. National Maritime
Museum, Greenwich.

The picture shows the old
'Leander' as a powder hulk at Upnor.

Only occasionally did he stray into historical painting, as in *The Battle of the Nile* of 1899, and his early work shows a strong feeling for composition and atmosphere. His later sea paintings and etchings always maintained a high level of achievement. His brother Charles

William Wyllie (1853–1923) was another accomplished sea painter. The sea attracted a number of subject painters, like James Clarke Hook (1819–1907), Stanhope Forbes (1857–1947), Henry Scott Tuke (1858–1929), a fine painter, who specialized in paint-

VII

PAINTERS ABROAD

When Queen Victoria came to the throne in 1837, her future Consort, on the advice of the King of the Belgians, was travelling diligently in and around Switzerland, since rumour had already linked their names together. Of the forty-four places he visited, he sent her views of all but two: from the Rigi he sent her an Alpenrose, and from Ferney a scrap of Voltaire's handwriting. By contemporary standards, particularly English ones, this enormous capacity for tourism was by no means exceptional. For by this year a great new age of travel had begun, as the where-abouts of some of the new Queen's subjects who earned a living by painting will show. After four years in Switzerland, Francis Danby was probably in Paris and due to embark on another four-year period of wandering about Europe. On his own in Italy since the age of fifteen, Alfred Stevens was learning to draw and paint, and, at the age of sixteen, Madox Brown was studying under Baron Wappers in Antwerp. George Chinnery, now somewhat overweight, was painting, 'taking snuff, smoking and snorting' in Macao, a thin sliver of land on the Chinese coast. James Holland had recently left Italy for Portugal, where he painted some of his finest water-colours. After some years of apprenticeship in Paris, William Callow was now established there as a teacher, and poised for a tour of Germany and Switzerland. Thomas Shotter Boys was working on his aseptically pure water-colours somewhere in France, while J. D. Harding was painting his way down the Rhine. Somewhere in Italy the comical figure of Edward Lear, with pebble glasses, protruberant nose and stomach, large beard and spindly legs, sitting astride a horse, swatting flies and cursing the discomfort and filth of village inns, must have appeared to startled natives as the embodiment of English eccentricity. This was his first journey abroad. In Italy, too, was another remarkable artist, Samuel Palmer, honey-mooning with Linnell's daughter, Hannah. Also with the Palmers were George Richmond and his wife.

Those about to pack their bags, lay in a stock of canvas and paint, and consult the steam-packet time-tables were John Frederick Lewis, who left in the following year for the Middle East, not to return for thirteen years; David Roberts, who, with a fine Scottish sense of economy, crammed all his Middle Eastern experience into two years, with rich results; the delicate William Müller, with only a few years to live, about to experience the ecstasy of Cairo, then an 'Arabian Nights' city; David Wilkie bound for the Middle East, never to return; John Ruskin, un-wontedly island-bound for a few years, about to issue forth on the series of tours which occupied him for nearly fifty years. Two years later, poor Richard Dadd also went to Egypt, where, it is said, he lost his reason while painting in the heat of the sun.

The age of the Grand Tour, a prerogative of the rich aristocracy, was nearly dead, for a new age of travel had been born in the 'thirties, more demo-cratised, more adventurous, and predominantly English. The opening of the Liverpool & Manchester Railway on 15th September, 1830, by the Duke of Wellington, caused a quickening of the pulse, trans-forming with great speed the habits of mankind. The Iron Duke himself soon came to regret that the rail-ways allowed the 'lower classes to travel about need-lessly', but within a few years England was covered by a web of railways. 'The early Scotchman', as Sydney Smith wrote, 'scratches himself in the morning mists of the north, and has his porridge in Piccadilly before the setting sun.' Soon the tentacles of the railway age spread to Europe: to France in 1832, to Belgium and Germany in 1835, to Austria in 1838, to Italy and Holland in 1839, to Switzerland in 1847 and to Spain in 1848. On the Continent, however, and particularly in France, the progress of the railways was spasmodic. In 1850 the traveller arriving by steamer at Calais, Havre, Brest or Bordeaux could not have continued by rail to any point on France's north-eastern, eastern or southern frontiers, whereas a traveller at Bremen or Hamburg could travel by rail direct to Cracow or Prague, and near to Cologne and Munich. By 1870, however, France under the Second Empire had man-aged to lay over 11,000 miles of rail. It was the same story with steamships. In 1816 England had fifteen steamships totalling 2,612 tons; by 1848 there were 1,253, totalling 168,078 tons. A contemporary jour-nalist wrote: 'we have reached in a single bound from the speed of a horse's canter, to the utmost speed comparable with the known strength and coherence of brass and iron' ('The Economist', January 1851). A guidebook of 1854 notes that 'splendid steam packets leave London Bridge for Calais, Boulogne and Havre almost every day'. Others 'start daily from Dover and Folkestone' and 'two or three times a week from Brighton to Dieppe, and from Southampton to Havre'. In the Balkans and Middle East such amenities were still rare. Edward Lear, attempting to describe a train and a steamboat to an ignorant Turkish Bey in the fortress town of Kroja, in Albania, resorted to imi-tating the noises they made. His performance—'Tik-tok, tik-tok, tik-tok, tokka, tokka, tokka, tokka - tok' (crescendo) and 'Squish-squash, squish-squash, squish-squash, thump-bump'—was so entertaining that the Bey demanded frequent encores.

The methods and conditions of travel in Europe, particularly where there were railways, were agree-able. Before the railways ousted them, the usual vehicles were diligences, mail-coaches, and post-carriages. In the backward Balkans and Middle East journeys 'are made only on horse-back', a means of transport highly extolled by one contemporary guidebook because 'there is none of that languor and feverishness that so generally result from travelling on wheels . . . You are in immediate contact with Nature.' Baedeker's guide for as late as 1876 confides bleakly that 'there are no railways in Syria'; and regrets that for long journeys through the desert there is no alternative to the camel, 'a sullen looking animal', whose dung 'is used in many parts of Syria as fuel'. Baedeker advises that 'on arrival at a Syrian port the traveller's passport is sometimes asked for, but an ordinary visiting-card will answer the purpose equally well', and devotes two closely printed pages to 'Intercourse with Orientals'. Murray's Handbook for Travellers in Greece for 1872 enjoins the traveller to follow 'the sensible recommendations of Mr Lear', and further warns him that 'Greece and all parts of the East abound in vermin of every description . . . some by their bite occasioning serious pain or illness'. Such, presumably, were those that elicited Lear's cry of anguish: 'O khan of Tirana! rats, mice, cockroaches, and all lesser vermin are there. Huge flimsy cobwebs, hanging in festoons above my head; big frizzly moths, bustling into my eyes and face.'

The majority of travellers to Europe and the Middle East were English. They swarmed everywhere. Switzerland, for example (which still had only 850 miles of railway system in 1870), could hardly contain the myriads of them. Johannes Brahms wrote to a friend in 1886 'It is magnificent here. Incidentally, there are many beer gardens where the English do not penetrate; for my comfort that is no small matter.' The domination of British tourists is implicit in contemporary phrase books ('I want to see the British Consul'). The English were blithely assured of their superiority, and the internal politics of countries they visited were beneath their contempt. If you should stumble on a Revolution, advised Walter Bagehot, there is no danger 'if you go calmly and look English'. Knowledge of the language was not considered a necessity: one English lady found she needed only two words of Italian, '*Quanto?*' and '*Troppo*'; and one gentleman considered that the one word '*Anglais*' met his needs throughout France.

Amongst the throng of tourists were large numbers of English artists touring Europe and the Orient in search of colour and exoticism. Some of these, like Holman Hunt, went in search of Scriptural subjects. Others, like Lewis, found their subjects in the bazaars of Cairo, or like Roberts, in ruins, churches, bedouins and their tents. Lear responded to strange, romantic scenery; Ruskin to mountains and church architecture. Sometimes the discomforts were appalling: 'the landscape painter', lamented Lear, 'has two alternatives; luxury and inconvenience on the one hand, liberty, hard living, and filth on the other; and of these two I chose the latter, as the most professionally

JOHN FREDERICK LEWIS,
R.A. *A Houri*. 30 × 25 inches. Mr
and Mrs Paul Mellon.

for *The Scapegoat*, was attacked by robbers near the Pools of Solomon on his way to Hebron; only after resolutely brandishing his revolver was he left in peace. Working away at *The Scapegoat* in the blazing sun, he was often harassed by hostile mounted Arab tribesmen 'their faces covered with black *kufeyiahs* and carrying long spears, while their footmen carried guns, swords and clubs'. The imperturbable artist placidly continued painting, steadying his touch by resting his hand on his double-barrelled gun. Further attacks on subsequent days were parried by threats of intervention by the British Consul. The Middle East was always close to turmoil. The Crimean war raged in the north, and it was while toiling away at *The Scapegoat* that Holman Hunt was brought news of the Battle of Inkerman. Eventually his courage and *sang-froid* so impressed the Arabs that they invited him to become their Sheikh. The picture itself was finally exhibited at the Royal Academy in 1856, after the death of two goats from exhaustion, and the use of a third. The reception of this picture, intended as it was to convey a symbolical message of 'the Church on Earth, subject to all the hatred of the unconverted world', was lukewarm. Indeed, to Ruskin 'it was a mere goat, with no more interest for us, than the sheep which furnished yesterday's dinner'.

On his first arrival in Cairo, Hunt had written to Millais complaining bitterly of his difficulty in getting Arab women to sit for him. Sometimes they were very beautiful, but more often than not they were inexpressibly ugly: when one of them finally deigned to remove her veil he 'discovered that nature had blessed her with some nasal departure from the monotony of ideal perfection.' Thomas Seddon (1821–1856) had accompanied Hunt on his journey to Palestine, without Hunt's high-minded devotional impulse, but partly through a wish to compensate for his own lack of any real training by 'novelty of motive', partly to observe closely Hunt's technical mastery, and partly to avoid working in his father's furniture business. After returning to England, he set out again for the East in 1856, only to die in the same year in Cairo, where he is buried. Further hazards of travel included the ever-present possibility of quarantine: David Roberts had once languished for thirty-five days in a kind of lazar house in Seville, because of a plague of cholera.

useful, though not the most agreeable' ('Journal of a landscape painter in Greece'). While painting in Albania, he was frequently pelted with stones by natives screaming '*Shaitan*' (devil), and by endless rain. When he visited Petra he came near to losing his life. A peace-loving man who, according to Holman Hunt, was as 'uncombative as a tender girl', he was surrounded by hysterical Arab robbers, manhandled, had his clothes torn, his beard pulled and his pockets picked of all they contained 'from dollars and penknives to handkerchiefs and hard-boiled eggs'. Reluctant to use his '5-barrelled revolver', he paid the marauders off with twenty dollars, and fled from the Wadi Mousa, only to be attacked again by large bands of *fellaheen*, who left him penniless. Holman Hunt, accompanied by the wretched animal which was to act as the model

Holman Hunt recalled of his first view of Cairo 'the interior of the bazaars, the streets, the mosques, the fountains, the tombs of the caliphs, the view from the Citadel, the avenues of lebek, the gates, old Cairo, all in turn offered a perfect subject for a painter of contemporary phases of Eastern life'. But he 'had no ambition to illustrate Cairo' and absorbed all that he saw 'to make the records of ancient history clearer'. It was left to painters like Lewis and Roberts to paint the scene before them.

John Frederick Lewis (1805–1876) is one of the most completely satisfying painters of the Victorian age. In a richly varied life, when he was either close to the top of the artistic Establishment of London, or idling among the fleshpots of Cairo, he managed to combine a degree of dedication to his calling with an artistry that showed no falling off as he grew older, so that when he was too weak to hold a brush he was able to say that it was the head that painted and not the hand. The eldest son of Frederick Christian Lewis, the engraver, was born, it is said, in the same house as Edwin Landseer, and began his artistic career by painting animals, a training which stood him in good stead in the Middle East. At the age of nineteen he published a set of six quarto plates of 'Studies of wild animals', thereby attracting the attention of George IV who employed him for some years to paint animals and sporting subjects in Windsor Park. So far, Lewis had confined himself to painting in oils. Having almost by accident become 'fascinated with the ease and with the simplicity of the tools required for working in water-colours', he soon became proficient in that medium. By 1829 he had become a full member of the Water-Colour Society. His first contact with the South came in 1832, on a two-year visit to Spain, which included a visit in the Spring of 1833 to Tangiers. Like John Phillip, he was stirred by Spain: its effect on his painting was galvanic, and from these years date the works of his maturity. His work began to be characterised by richness of colour and closeness of observation. He rendered warm tints with careful stippling and the use of body-colour for the high-lights. His fame began to spread, earning him the nickname 'Spanish Lewis', and was further enhanced by the publication of two volumes of lithographs, 'Sketches and Drawings of the Alhambra' (1835) and 'Lewis's Sketches of Spain and Spanish Character' (1836).

At this point the smooth progress of his career became erratic. In 1839 the secretary of the Water-Colour Society received a letter from Lewis 'dated from Rome' to say that illness and other circum-

THOMAS SEDDON. *Jerusalem and the Valley of Jehoshaphat from the Hill of Evil Counsel*. Body-colour. $9\frac{1}{2} \times 12\frac{1}{8}$ inches. John Gere, Esq.
This is a smaller version of the picture, now at the Tate Gallery, which Seddon painted over a period of five months in 1854. Another yet smaller version, which belonged to Rossetti and was said by him to have been painted over a photograph, is at the Ashmolean (see Chapter 13).

stances prevented him from exhibiting that year. However in 1841 he sent in two pictures, including apparently *Easter Day at Rome*, his only work done in Italy. Nothing more was heard from him until 1844, and then it was from Cairo. In fact, Lewis was absent from England for thirteen years. He had apparently gone from Paris to Rome, then on to Corfu, Albania, Athens and Constantinople, finally reaching Cairo in the winter of 1842. From there, when his lethargy permitted, he made occasional sorties up the Nile into Nubia. It was in Cairo that his old friend, the novelist Thackeray, paid him a visit. Thackeray discovered him in a 'long, queer, many-windowed, many galleried house', with a great hall of audience, its ceiling 'embroidered with arabesques'. This house, with its divans and fountains, was 'more sumptuously furnished' than the houses of the 'Beys and Agas his neighbours'. Here, amidst the pipe-bringing servants, Lewis was an exotic host, in a dark blue costume with embroidered jacket, his beard curling nobly over his chest, his Damascus scimitar on his thigh. 'Here he lives like a languid lotus-eater—a dreamy, hazy, lazy, tobaccofied life', wrote Thackeray.

Meanwhile, in London, Lewis's long absence caused his name to be struck off the list of members of the Water-Colour Society. On hearing of this he wrote begging to be re-instated, and this was done; and he caused a sensation at the exhibition in 1850 with *The Hhareem*. Its high finish and brilliance of colouring caused the public to place him with the Pre-Raphaelites, although he had never met any members of The Brotherhood. In 1851 Lewis returned, and until his death continued to exhibit his eastern scenes. In Cairo he had again taken up oil-painting, which gave his pictures, as the Redgraves wrote, 'a richness of colouring and a brilliant perfection of completeness which seem almost peculiar to himself; his drawing is so exceedingly accurate, and his manual dexterity so great, that he is able to combine the utmost finish without oppressing you with any sense of the labour of execution.' It is in this last respect that Lewis's technique is superior to that of most of the more self-conscious Pre-Raphaelites, and none of his contemporaries could equal his treatment of brilliant colours seen through a diffused light. He became President of the Water-Colour Society in 1855, to resign two years later in favour of an almost total commitment to oils. He had already been elected R.A. His industry as a painter was exceptional: he would start work at eight and work without interruption throughout the

JOHN FREDERICK LEWIS, R.A. *Two Women in a Harem*. Pencil, water-colour and body-colour. 14 × 17½ inches. Charles Jerdein, Esq.

day, taking tremendous trouble in the preparation of his colours, which were mostly mineral and were chosen with great care. He painted with very small sable brushes, using hog's hair brushes only for backgrounds or for scrubbing in. Lewis fully deserved the panegyric that Ruskin gave him in the Academy Notes of 1856: 'Labour thus concentrated in large purpose—detail thus united into effective mass—has not been seen till now.' Most refreshingly and strikingly, his pictures are entirely free of anecdote, cloying sentiment or moral fervour, thus marking him as a forerunner of the aesthetic movement.

Lewis was one of the last artists to see Sir David Wilkie alive; he had met him in Constantinople and seen him leave for Cairo. Wilkie had been turning over in his mind for some time the possibility of doing some biblical painting, derived not from imagination but from observation, a motive curiously similar to that of Holman Hunt, but without Hunt's high religious purpose. In the Autumn of 1840, he decided to go to the Middle East, leaving behind him a trail of commissions and uncompleted portraits. He spoke to his friend William Collins on the eve of departure of 'the advantage he might derive from painting upon Holy Land, on the very ground on which the event he was to embody had actually occurred'. By way of The Hague, Cologne, Munich and Vienna, he reached Constantinople in October 1840. Here he was delayed for five months because of the war between Turkey

JOHN FREDERICK LEWIS, R.A. *The Prayer of Faith.* Watercolour. 23 × 17¾ inches. Signed and dated 1872. Charles Jerdein, Esq.
Exhibited at the Paris Universal Exhibition 1878.

and Syria, but he was able to paint some lovely watercolour sketches and a fine portrait of the Turkish Sultan. After further irritating delays caused by plagues and quarantine, he reached Jerusalem. Here he did some more fine water-colour sketches, which were never worked-up. Then he sailed on a steamer with a cargo of soap for Alexandria, where he had time to paint another exquisite portrait, this time of Muhemed Ali. According to Benjamin Robert Haydon, who had talked to William Woodburn, one of the last to see Wilkie alive, 'he quacked himself to death; his

JOHN SCARLETT DAVIS. *The Art Gallery of the Farnese Palace, Parma.* 38¼ × 73¼ inches. Initialled, inscribed 'Parma', and dated 1839. Marchioness of Dufferin and Ava.

only anxiety wherever he went was, if there was a medical man in town'. Wilkie left Alexandria for England on the 'Oriental' steamer, and he soon had attacks of illness, exacerbated by rashly eating fruits and ices in Malta harbour. He grew steadily worse and died at sea the next day, 1st June, 1841. In the evening his body 'was committed to the deep with all due rites and honours', an event which was to be immortalised in Turner's *Peace – Burial at Sea.*

John Scarlett Davis (1804–1845), a native of Hereford, pursued a solitary course, painting numerous interiors of Italian churches and museums, reproducing the Old Master paintings on their walls with extraordinary fidelity. Like Bonington, who was two years his senior, he had studied at the Louvre, which may account for a certain apparent similarity in their work.

William Müller made three separate journeys abroad during Queen Victoria's reign. The first, in 1838, took him through Greece to Egypt, where David Roberts was also at work; in 1840 he toured northern and central France, staying for a while in Paris; in 1843 he joined a party bound for the Middle East, this time going to Smyrna and Rhodes. Although the effect on his style of painting was, to a degree, predictable, he lacked the judgment and refinement of Lewis and the control of Roberts. His palette became richer and the chiaroscuro stronger, but too often one feels that he had looked too long at Rembrandt and Delacroix, and not long enough at his subject: his exuberant style often degenerates into a mire of coagulated colour and the delicacy he showed in his water-colours escaped him. However, works like *An Eastern Street Scene* at the Tate Gallery show the redeeming qualities of ordered composition and a fine colour sense.

A more disciplined artist was David Roberts (1796–1864), who has been called 'the Scottish Canaletto' (another case of that curious inferiority complex with which the British regard their artists). Roberts was born at Stockbridge, near Edinburgh, the son of a poor shoemaker. After a seven-year apprenticeship to a house-painter in Edinburgh, he took up scene painting. It was at the Theatre Royal, Edinburgh, that he first met Clarkson Stanfield, with whom he formed a life-long friendship. Both painters came to London in 1822, and soon after their arrival worked together at the Drury Lane Theatre, at the same time busily painting easel pictures and exhibiting at the Royal Academy. In 1826 Roberts became scene painter at Covent Garden Theatre, and designed and painted the sets for the first London production of Mozart's 'Il Seraglio'. Three years later Roberts went abroad for the first of many tours. In 1830 he got as far as Cologne, but turned back because of political disturbances there. Two years later he set off, on the advice of Wilkie, for another tour of France and Spain, visiting Tangiers and Morocco. If he was cool about Spanish cooking ('Between oil and garlic it is difficult to tell what you are eating'), he was enthusiastic about the architecture, and made over 250 sketches; working these up occupied him for the next four years. In 1838, by way of France, Italy and Malta, he arrived again in the Middle East. On his arrival in Egypt he dined with the British Consul in Alexandria, who arranged for him to travel up the Nile to Ethiopia. He spent the next year in Palestine, dressed as an Arab, painting and drawing industriously. On his return to England in 1840 he found, with some difficulty, a publisher for his drawings. The fruits of his labours were published in the six volume 'Views in the Holy Land, Syria, Idumea, Arabia, Egypt and Nubia' (1842–9). After being elected R.A. he resumed his travels—to Northern France in 1843, Belgium in 1844–5, to both these countries again in 1849, Italy and Austria in 1851, Italy again in 1851 and lastly Belgium in 1862. He spent the last four years of his life painting a series of pictures called 'London from the River Thames'.

Like Lewis, Roberts was very prolific: for nearly thirty years he rarely failed to exhibit at the Royal Academy. The works of his maturity fall into three distinct groups: from 1838 to 1848, Spanish; from 1851 to 1860, Italian; and from 1860 to 1864, London. And yet his style varied little. The subtle whiff of local flavour captured by Lewis often eluded Roberts: not for want of accuracy—he employed pencil and ruler, like an architect, on his canvas—and the groups of figures are always spirited, and carefully placed;

yet somehow, whether he is in Luxor or Venice, the colouring belongs to Roberts, not to the locality. However, there is a kind of stringent professionalism and purity of vision about his work which compels admiration.

If the coolness of Roberts's artistic vision remained constant on his first contact with the warm south, that of his fellow Scotsman, John Phillip (1817–1867) burst into colourful bloom, burgeoning with warmth and life. Phillip was an original member of the Clique, together with Egg, Dadd, O'Neil and Frith, and his earlier works were, by general consent, anaemic imitations of David Wilkie. Born in Aberdeen and, like Roberts, the son of a shoemaker, he began his working life as an errand boy to a tinsmith. An early

Opposite page, below:
WILLIAM JAMES MÜLLER. *An Eastern Street Scene.* 23¾ × 35½ inches. Tate Gallery, London.

DAVID ROBERTS, R.A. *Gateway of the Great Temple at Baalbek.* 29½ × 24½ inches. Royal Academy, London.
Painted in the winter of 1842 and exhibited at the Royal Academy in 1843. Roberts wrote in his diary on 2nd May, 1839 his first impressions of Baalbek: 'have begun my studies of the temple, of the magnificence of which it is impossible to convey any idea, either by pencil or pen. The beauty of its form, the exquisite richness of its ornament, and the vast magnitude of its dimensions, are altogether unparalleled.'

JOHN PHILLIP, R.A. *La Gloria*. 56½ × 85½ inches. Signed with monogram and dated 1864. National Gallery of Scotland, Edinburgh.

Exhibited at the Royal Academy in 1864. The artist considered this his best picture.

Opposite page, below:
FREDERICK GOODALL, R.A. *Early Morning in the Wilderness of Shur*. 56 × 134 inches. Signed and dated 1860. Guildhall Art Gallery, London.

Exhibited at the Royal Academy in 1860. An Arab sheikh is addressing his tribe, on breaking up their encampment at the 'Well of Moses' on the eastern shore of the Red Sea.

enthusiasm for painting brought him to London and eventually, in 1837, to the Royal Academy Schools. Two years later he returned to Aberdeen where he remained for some years painting portraits and Highland genre scenes. Delicate health prompted his first visit to Spain in 1851; he settled at Seville, and the inhibitions which had constricted his development evaporated in the sun. The gaiety, animal vigour, colourful clothing and festive nature of the Spaniards inspired his painting. His figures became flesh and blood, his composition lively, his colours richer and brighter, although he was not yet adept at modulating them carefully over relatively large areas. His technique improved on acquaintance with the paintings of Velasquez and Murillo. Soon his Spanish pictures began to appear at the Royal Academy and he acquired the nickname 'Spanish Phillip'. In 1856 he paid his second visit to Spain, accompanied by Richard Ansdell. A year after being elected R.A.

in 1859, he visited Spain for the third and last time: going farther afield, he saw Madrid, Segovia, Toledo, Cordova and Seville, studying Velasquez again, and copying him. From this time onwards he painted some of his finest pictures, with complete assurance of handling, the colours even richer and more subtly modulated. Pictures like *La Bomba* and *La Gloria* (by which Phillip expressly asked that his achievement should be judged) are characteristic of his best period. He visited Rome in 1866, and died shortly afterwards.

In 1854 war broke out between the Russia of Tsar Nicholas I, Tennyson's 'icy Muscovite', on the one side and Palmerston's England, Napoleon III's France, and Turkey, on the other. After two years of fighting, where disease vied with the battlefield as the most potent destroyer of soldiers, the Treaty of Paris finally secured for the Western allies the terms for which they had professed to contend. Wars supplied artists with some useful subject matter – then, and for some years to come: notably for paintings like Henry O'Neil's *Eastward Ho!* and *Home Again*. The Light Brigade charged again and again on canvas and in picture-books. More interesting, though, was the arrival on the scene of the first war-photographer, Roger Fenton, and the first two war-artists, William Simpson (1823–1899) and Edward Angelo Goodall (1819–1908). Both are rather minor artists, and best known in water-colour. Simpson devoted forty years of his life to painting wars. He was first commissioned to paint scenes in the Crimea. Eighty of these appeared as chromo-lithographs in 'The Seat of the War in the East' (1855). He also painted a picture of Balaclava for the Queen. After the war he joined the Duke of Newcastle's party which explored Circassia. In 1859, soon after the first Indian Mutiny, he was commissioned by a firm of publishers to paint scenes in India. Subsequently we find him on the staff of 'The Illustrated London News', travelling to Abyssinia and India. The Franco-Prussian War of 1870 and the Afghan war eight years later provided him with further material.

E. A. Goodall was one of a large family of artists. In 1841 he accompanied the Schomburgk Guiana Boundary Expedition as draughtsman, exhibiting a picture painted in British Guiana at the Royal Academy four years later. On the outbreak of the Crimean war he was sent by 'The Illustrated London News', to which he sent back numerous sketches: these were swiftly engraved on wood-blocks to be studied avidly by the Victorian public. After this Goodall went further afield and painted delicate water-colours in Italy and Egypt. Frederick Goodall (1822–1904), his younger brother, exhibited an enormous number of Eastern scenes at the Royal Academy for forty-two years, bearing such titles as *Bedouin Mother and Child*—

Afterglow and *An Intruder on the Bedouin's Pasture*: in their almost unrelieved tedium, they are a long way from the splendours of J. F. Lewis.

The topographical tradition in water-colour painting of Thomas Malton and Edward Dayes persisted until the death of William Callow (b. 1812) in 1908. He, Thomas Shotter Boys (1803–1874) and James Holland (1800–1870) were cast in the mould of Bonington. Indeed, Boys had known Bonington in Paris, and may have studied under him. Callow met

JOHN PHILLIP, R.A. *A Chat round the Brasero.* 36 × 48 inches. Initialled and dated 1866. Guildhall Art Gallery, London.

Exhibited at the Royal Academy, in 1866. 'Spanish' Phillip died within a year of exhibiting this picture.

JAMES HOLLAND. *View of the Rialto Bridge, Venice.* 38 × 58 inches. Signed and dated 1859. Fine Art Society, London.

Exhibited at Manchester in the Royal Jubilee Exhibition in 1887.

Opposite page:
EDWARD LEAR. *Kangchenjunga.* 15 × 8¾ inches. Private collection, London.

Painted in 1880. Lear was commissioned by Lord Northbrook to do a large picture of this subject. Lear wrote of this mountain on the Nepal/Sikkim frontier: '[It is] not —so it seems to me—a sympathetic mountain; it is so far off, so very God-like and stupendous'.

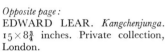

EDWARD PRITCHETT. *Doge's Palace, Venice.* 20 × 16 inches. Signed. G. Berge, Esq.

Boys, a 'clever but eccentric artist' on his second visit to Paris in 1831 and learnt a great deal of the theory and practice of art from him, 'and it was from him', he wrote, 'I first acquired my love for making water-colour drawings of picturesque old churches and houses, for which subjects I have had a partiality ever since'. Subjects like these, together with landscapes, were to form the main body of their work. James Holland, who was born two years before Bonington and began his career by painting flowers in James Davenport's factory, was another who followed in the steps of Bonington. His views of Venice, many dashingly painted in oils with an adventurous use of colour, show an assurance of manner which suggests a further debt to Turner. Edward Pritchett (exhib. 1828–1864) was also attracted to Venice: his views of the city, in both oils and water-colour, were exhibited regularly at the Royal Academy and then the British Institution; the influences on him were clearly similar to those on James Holland. Although he was largely repetitive, some of his work indicates a strong talent for the picturesque. The cream of this group's achievement, however, lies in the best water-colours of Boys, Callow and Holland, which, as worthy successors to the work of Bonington, assured the continuing strength of the English water-colour tradition. Another august name in this tradition was Samuel Prout

(1783–1852), whose water-colours of crumbling stone and brick buildings in Northern Europe excited the reverence of Victorians and the not uncritical adulation of Ruskin; a pupil of Prout, James Duffield Harding (1797–1863), described by Ruskin as 'brilliant and vigorous', is another agreeable draughtsman, highly esteemed by Victorians, but now considered an artist of only moderate talent.

In a rather turgid account of the geological structure of land and seascape throughout the world in a series in 'The Art Journal' of 1863, the geologist David Ansted attempted to supply a scientific gloss to Ruskin's exhortations concerning Truth in Art. The author observed that 'all appreciation of grand scenery dates from a very recent period . . . the recognition of any real beauty and interest in mountainous and wild countries was hardly ever made, even a century ago—being as much a growth of modern taste and modern cultivation as are the novel, and other peculiarities of literary composition'. He went on to note that mountains and difficult terrain up to a short time before were avoided wherever possible; this no longer being the case, he analysed their 'physiognomy and characteristic features', as an aid to the artist. One artist who surely benefited by Professor Ansted's advice was Elijah Walton (1833–1880) whose precisely geological water-colour views of the Alps are among his best works. If there was one individual who would have profited little by Ansted's series of articles, it was Edward Lear (1812–1888). No artist understood the geological characteristics of strange and wild landscapes so well, and no other artist had travelled as extensively over so many years as Lear, who observed and recorded in water-colour and oils on a prodigious scale. Lear was the second youngest of twenty-one children, brought up in a fair degree of comfort, only to be forced to earn a living at the age of fifteen, through the imprisonment of his father for bankruptcy. After being taught to draw by his sister, Sarah, he was able to obtain freelance work. Shortly after this, he began to draw in the Zoological Gardens.

From his first tour of the Continent in 1837 until his death at San Remo in 1888, Lear was hardly ever still. With his restless passion for work, his curiosity, his nervous condition—he was subject to mild epileptic seizures, sometimes as many as eighteen in a month—he traversed Europe and Asia, usually alone, but in later years with his man-servant Kokali. Writing letters to his sister, Ann, to relatives and friends, keeping his Journals, and painting, he was in as many as five or six countries a year, from the Lowlands to Prague, to Vienna, Dubrovnik, Albania, Greece, Palestine, Egypt, Sicily, Italy, France and England. The years 1873 to 1875 saw him in India and Ceylon, at first delirious with 'violent and amazing delight at the wonderful varieties of life and dress here', drawing

Forest of Bavella, Corsica by Edward Lear is reproduced in colour on p. 108.

and painting feverishly; finally weary of 'this most miserable Indian journey', he sailed for Brindisi. The last years of his life were spent at San Remo, where he died far from his many friends.

Lear's painting was always inspired by the romantic element in landscape. Jagged mountains, huge trees, distant views at sunset, precipices, ravines: these he treated with a technical skill and a character absolutely unique to him. The structure of his water-colours is predominantly linear, and in his oil-paintings his handling of paint is at times almost abstract: an oil sketch by Lear can resemble the work of Sidney Nolan. A Pre-Raphaelite influence, by reason of his association with Holman Hunt in the 'fifties, is also discernible: the mountainous back-ground to *The Scapegoat* looks as though it might have been painted by Lear. Mr Brian Reade, in his introduction to the Lear Exhibition at the Arts Council in 1958, gave a vivid account of Lear's methods: 'He would set out with his gear and his manservant, select a site, lift his spectacles, gaze at the scene before him through a monocular glass, and then, readjusting his spectacles, begin to draw rapidly in pencil. Certain details would be inscribed in longhand with colour notes in Lear's own special phonetic spelling, "rox" for rocks, "ski" for sky, and so on. Sometimes he would apply water-colour in generalized tints over large areas with great dash. Much of this work must have been done indoors. In the evenings too he would "pen over" the pencil and water-colour sketches, graduating minutely the receding planes and out-lining the forms rather sharply, so as to give an effect of crystalline elegance.' Lear's work undoubtedly suffered from over-production, but no one would have been more surprised than he to learn that he is now considered, and rightly so, to be one of the most original landscape painters of the nineteenth century, standing fully in the tradition of Martin and Danby.

For sheer prodigality of character, career and production it would be hard to find another artist to equal George Chinnery (1774–1852): of his total span of seventy-eight years, the last fifty were spent entirely in the Far East, for reasons that were, at least at first, more matrimonial than artistic; and, oils apart, his vivid drawings and water-colours are only exceeded in number and fluency by Rowlandson's. Chinnery's father, who was of East Anglian stock, was an amateur painter, who encouraged his son to paint and draw at an early age. In 1791, Chinnery was a contemporary of Turner at the Royal Academy Schools; Sir Joshua Reynolds, then President, died the following year.

When he was only seventeen, he exhibited a

EDWARD LEAR. *Dubrovnik, Yugoslavia.* Pen, ink and water-colour. 13½ × 21 inches. Mrs E. P. Card. Annotated, inscribed and dated 'Ragusa, 6 a.m. 5th May, 9 a.m., 5 p.m. 6th May 1866 (43)'.

portrait, and portraiture continued to prove a lucrative mainstay for the rest of his life. This portraiture always betrayed an early debt to Reynolds and Romney, just as his pencil and wash groups show the influence of Cosway. For the next four years he exhibited a succession of portraits at the Royal Academy, until, at the suggestion of an influential uncle, Sir Broderick Chinnery, he crossed over to Dublin. Here he was the guest of James Vigne, a jeweller, whose daughter, Marianne, he married in 1799. In Dublin he painted a number of miniatures, showing the effect of his contact with John Comerford the miniaturist, and his first landscapes; it was in the Irish capital that he left a durable mark, the revival of the dormant Society of Arts in Ireland. Three years later he returned to England with his wife and two children, to live at Gilwell Park, Essex. It seems that extravagance and a wayward nature were by now contributing to a breakdown in his marriage, and he seized the first opportunity to sail for India, where he arrived later in the same year. He remained for twenty-three years, living mostly in Calcutta. There he became a well-known figure with the British Raj, undertaking a number of portrait commissions—he was reputedly earning up to £500 a month—and filling hundreds of sketchbooks with brilliantly observed scenes of Indian life. He was 'the ablest limner in the land' according to his friend Sir Charles D'Oyly, and he devoted his leisure to 'smoky meditation'—

assuredly a reference to an addiction to opium. This opium dream was rudely awakened by the successive arrivals of his daughter, his wife and his son. Chinnery tried to keep up appearances for a time in spite of the existence of two illegitimate sons by an unknown mother; then, in his own words, 'he had to bolt for China for £40,000 of debt'. 'To get so heavily involved', a contemporary commented, 'is a sign of his genius.'

In the early summer of 1825, at the age of fifty, he reached Macao where he remained, occasionally visiting Canton and Hongkong, until his death. His wife followed him about four years later, but he took refuge in Canton, where he thanked providence for the 'Chinese government that forbids the softer sex from coming and bothering us here'. Mrs Chinnery was accordingly refused permission to disembark and, languishing on board the ship, she caught smallpox and died. From now on Chinnery settled into a comfortable pattern of life drinking vast quantities of tea, and eating so much that four bearers were needed to carry his personal chair around the alleyways of Macao; making innumerable drawings of the Chinese going about their daily tasks, water-colour views, and oil-paintings of English and Chinese officials, views of Macao, junks and market scenes. Although never allowing his work to become orientalised, he founded what has become known as a 'Chinnery School'. He employed a number of assis-

Dent's Verandah, Macao by George Chinnery is reproduced in colour on p. 117.

GEORGE CHINNERY. *Portraits of Sir Jamsetjee Jejeebhoy and a Man Servant* (detail). $28\frac{1}{2} \times 21\frac{3}{4}$ inches. John Keswick, Esq., C.M.G.

Sir Jamsetjee Jejeebhoy was a prominent Parsee merchant from Bombay. He was said to have made a fortune from the sale of opium. He was also a great benefactor and was made a baronet by Queen Victoria. It seems likely, since he has a Chinese manservant, that the picture was painted while he was on a visit to Macao.

tants and copyists, whose names sound like a jingle from 'The Mikado'—Protin Qua, Sun Qua, Fal Qua, Tin Qua, Yin Qua and Lam Qua. Lam Qua acquired a certain status by actually sending pictures for exhibition at the Royal Academy. Chinnery mixed and ground his own pigments, and used thin canvases of local manufacture. He was fond of vermilion, using dabs of it for eyes, lips, nostrils and ears; and Chinese white for flecks of light in the landscapes. He continued to send pictures to the Royal Academy until his death from apoplexy in 1852. Chinnery occupies a special place in Victorian painting: not only was he the only important European artist of the time to live and work in the Far East for the greater part of his life, but his paintings, in oils and water-colour, and his drawings have a vigorous and fluent character entirely their own, earning the praise of Sir Francis Chantrey who said that he never saw a figure drawn by Chinnery that he 'could not cut a statue from'.

VIII

EARLY GENRE

Reviewing the Royal Academy Exhibition in June 1863, 'The Art Journal' critic, to avoid discussing the pictures room by room, decided to 'distribute under distinct headings the diversified works here thrown confusedly together'. It is no surprise that the first division consisted of 'HIGH ART: HISTORY—SACRED AND SECULAR.' This section contains some engaging titles: *La Toilette des Morts*, 'an incident in the tragic life of Charlotte Corday' by E. M. Ward; *The Power of Music*, by H. N. O'Neil, a sequel to his successful *Mozart on his Death-bed giving Directions for the Performance of his last Requiem* and, selected for praise by the reviewer, *Robespierre receiving Letters from the Friends of his Victims which threaten him with Assassination*, by William Henry Fisk (1827–1884). One is momentarily startled to see the name of Leighton appearing in such company. The next category in descending order is 'SUBJECTS POETIC AND IMAGINATIVE'. Here there are Millais's *The Eve of St. Agnes*, with its vestigial Pre-Raphaelitism and *My First*

Sermon, his earliest experiment in the sentimental treatment of childhood, which was commended by the Archbishop of Canterbury whose spirit was 'touched by the playfulness, the innocence, the purity, and may I not add, the piety of childhood'; William Powell Frith (1819–1909) is represented by *Juliet*, his *Derby Day* being five years behind him; Paul Falconer Poole (1807–1879) shows a pastoral scene with amorous peasants. Henry William Pickersgill (1782–1875) shows *Desdemona's Intercession for Cassio*, while Frederick Richard Pickersgill (1820–1900) has *Ferdinand and Miranda;* and the reviewer notes 'the tender refinement' of *Hermione* by William Maw Egley (1826–1916). The next division is 'PORTRAITS', where the reviewer confesses to bewilderment 'at the inordinate number of them'. Then, noting that 'England, happy in her homes, and joyous in her hearty cheer, and peaceful in her snug firesides, is equally fortunate in a school of Art sacred to the hallowed relations of domestic life', he reaches 'SCENES DOMESTIC—

SIR DAVID WILKIE, R.A. *The Bride at her Toilet*. 38¼ × 48¼ inches. National Gallery of Scotland, Edinburgh.

Exhibited at the Royal Academy in 1838. Thackeray wrote of it: 'The colour of this picture is delicious, and the effect faultless: Sir David does everything for a picture nowadays but the *drawing*. Who knows? Perhaps it is as well left out.'

GRAVE AND GAY'. To this category he appends 'OUT-DOOR FIGURES—RUDE, RUSTIC AND REFINED', with the lame explanation that 'the experience of the kitchen and the parlour finds its correspondence in the incidents of the field or the garden'. The list ends with animal, fruit and flower, sea and landscape painting.

This second hierarchical exercise in grading the subjects of art, coming twenty-five years after Thackeray's, besides stressing the nagging Victorian obsession with subject matter, affords a useful glimpse of a typical exhibition nearly at mid-point in the reign of Queen Victoria. At first sight it would appear to differ little from an exhibition of 1837. But the Royal Academy in 1863 had been through the fire of Pre-Raphaelitism, the embers of which still glowed; historical painting was now fused with subjects from Northern and Southern mythology; Roberts, Lewis and Goodall were sending in exotic Eastern subjects; the neo-classical influence was making itself felt: genre was creeping into the marbled palaces of Greece and Rome. Hierarchy of subject apart, it is clear, however, that by far the greatest number of pictures are of domestic scenes, in or out of doors, often with an anecdotal interest, sometimes from contemporary life and at other times from history and literature, and often thickly coated with sentiment. 'They are subjects', wrote Henry James, 'addressed to a taste of a particularly unimaginative and unaesthetic order—to the taste of the British merchant and paterfamilias and his excellently regulated family. What this taste appears to demand of a picture is that it shall have a taking title, like a three-volume novel or an article in a magazine: that it shall embody in its lower flights some comfortable incident of the daily life of our period, suggestive more especially of its gentilities and proprieties and familiar moralities.'

Among the many thousands of Victorian painters who practised genre painting, most are now forgotten, while some are remembered only for a few paintings of a very high order; some few, like W. P. Frith, could devote a lifetime to genre painting, and rarely turn out a bad picture. It was only comparatively recently that Mr Graham Reynolds sympathetically drew our attention to their productions, and new discoveries are coming to light all the time. The main appeal these paintings now have for us is their simple charm, their value as documents of social interest and, more often than is sometimes acknowledged, their painterly qualities. The frequent charge that one genre painting is very like another, while containing an element of truth, arises usually out of a lack of sympathy for the subject. Never before had an age been visually so well documented.

This kind of painting had been popular in England since the time of Hogarth, but it was David Wilkie

(1785–1841), 'a raw tall, pale, queer Scotsman', who established its ascendancy in Victorian England. Although he survived the Queen's accession for only five years, the last two of which were spent in the Middle East (from which he never returned), his influence pervaded painting throughout her reign. Ironically, Wilkie's own personal reputation was in decline by 1837. His great successes lay far behind him: coming to London in May 1805, 'he saw a picture of Teniers', in the words of Sir George Beaumont, 'and at once painted *The Village Politicians*'. The Dutch

SIR DAVID WILKIE, R.A. *The Empress Josephine and the Fortune-Teller*. 83 × 62 inches. Signed and dated 1837. National Gallery of Scotland, Edinburgh.
Exhibited at the Royal Academy in 1837. The picture illustrates an incident in Martinique, the Empress Josephine's native island, when a negress read in the palm of her hand that she would one day be crowned and be greater than a Queen.

WILLIAM MULREADY, R.A.
Crossing the Ford. Panel. 24×20
inches. Tate Gallery, London.
Exhibited at the Royal Academy
in 1842.

Below right:
CHARLES BAXTER. *The Pretty
Peasant*. 14×12 inches. Guildhall
Art Gallery, London.

model was already evident in the early *Pitlassie Fair*. These early works were followed by the immensely popular *Blind Fiddler*, *The Village Festival*, *Blindman's Buff*, and the highly esteemed *Reading the Gazette of the Battle of Waterloo* of 1822. Wilkie's dominance in genre was then supreme. While his earlier work wore a brighter plumage (C. L. Nursey, a pupil of Wilkie, described to Holman Hunt how his master had painted *The Blind Fiddler* 'without any dead colouring, finishing each bit thoroughly in the day'), his later work became broader and darker, with the use of bitumen working its usual havoc. It also became more international in style, more heroic, although to Thackeray his pictures seemed 'to be painted with snuff and tallow-grease'. Tragically teetering on the edge of the abyss of High Art, he went to Palestine in search of material for biblical paintings, anticipating a similar quest by Holman Hunt nearly twenty-five years later. He had visited Madrid in 1827, the first of a long line of painters including Roberts, Lewis and Phillip, to do so. But it was the genre pictures of his early and middle period, together with those of his rival William Mulready (1786–1863), which determined the course of Victorian subject painting. The subject-matter of his pictures was already tending towards children and dogs set in simple domestic surroundings. Although never mawkish, Mulready's pictures tended, more than Wilkie's, to sentiment. During the latter half of the century sentimentality, the right wing of hypocrisy, swelled from a thin coat to a thick sludge: Mulready died in the year in which Millais's *My First Sermon* was exhibited at the Royal Academy.

Like Wilkie, Mulready was already an established figure long before 1837. After an early career as a landscape painter of some sensitivity, he was, from 1807, converted by the example of Wilkie to genre painting. Again the grouping is reminiscent of Ostade and Teniers. But he was not what Horace Walpole called one of those 'drudging Mimicks of Nature's most uncomely coarsenesses', but an observer of rare talent. Although his pictures never acquired the same individual fame as Wilkie's, there is a greater consistency about his painting which never degenerates into monotony. Mulready, moreover, was a great colourist. Never darkening his canvases with bitumen, he painted as the Pre-Raphaelites did later, in thin glazes over a white ground, achieving a transparent luminosity of colour. Four years before the foundation of the Brotherhood, Thackeray noted his 'brilliant, rich, astonishingly luminous and intense' colours.

Not unlike Mulready was Thomas Webster (1800–1886), whose best-known picture is *The Village Choir*, at the Victoria and Albert Museum. His studies of schoolboy pranks are genuinely humorous and never treacly. The same cannot be said of the 'dangerous smiling Delilahs' painted by artists like Edmund Thomas Parris (1793–1873), Charles Baxter (1809–1879) and Frank Stone (1800–1859). Hovering on the brink of genre painting, they are merely a framed version of 'The Keepsake' beauties. While its artistic

Opposite page, above right:
WILLIAM MULREADY, R.A. *The Younger Brother.* 30½ × 24¾ inches. Tate Gallery, London.

Exhibited at the Royal Academy in 1857. Commissioned by Robert Vernon, but not finished until eight years after Vernon's death. A reviewer of the Academy exhibition in 'The Art Journal' noted that 'there is no narrative, no allusive incident; the beauty and power of the work lie in its execution and colour – the former is marvellously minute, the latter brilliant and most harmonious'. Ruskin considered it 'without exception, the least interesting piece of good painting I have ever seen in my life' (Academy Notes).

DAVID ROBERTS, R.A. *Cathedral and Piazza at Brescia, Lombardy.* 21½ × 35½ inches. Signed and dated 1860. Major and Mrs Angus Rowan-Hamilton.

Painted for the dealer, Flatow, for the sum of £157 10s. See p. 95.

EDWARD LEAR. *Forest of Bavella, Corsica.* 57½×95 inches. Alexander Martin, Esq.

Lear was in Corsica in 1868. This picture probably dates from 1878-80, and is said to have been bought by the Earl of Derby, the son of his first patron. Lear made a number of sketches of Bavella, which made a deep impression on him. He wrote in his diary on 29th April 1868: 'a painter . . . might and should endure anything short of starvation, to see what I have seen of Bavella'. *See p. 100.*

value amounts to very little, this kind of painting retains for us a certain period charm. Far more interesting are the figure sketches of William Henry Hunt (1790–1864); always painted in delicate stippled water-colours, they depict amusing scenes from everyday life. His single figure studies are painted with an exquisite under-statement, rare at the time. E. M. Ward is an instance of an historical painter, who, taking time off from the onerous rigours of painting on a large scale, could depict delightful little scenes from everyday life. William Gush (exhib. 1833–1874) was an aptly named portraitist of some charm, whose portraits were painted in 'The Keepsake' tradition.

In 1843 appeared Mulready's illustrations to 'The Vicar of Wakefield', published by Van Voorst. They coincided with the rise of a school of historical genre painting, which up till the end of the century was to engage the talents of subject painters. Charles Robert Leslie (1794–1859) was the first of a line that ended with Seymour Lucas, G. D. Leslie, F. W. Topham and others. Most of the subjects were drawn from

literature: the works of Cervantes, Molière, Shakespeare and Goldsmith being the most popular. Easily topping the list was the 'Vicar of Wakefield'. William Powell Frith was one of the first to illustrate the work of a contemporary novelist, in 1842, with the subject of Dolly Varden from Dickens's 'Barnaby Rudge' which was published in the same year, although the novel is set in the age of Goldsmith. In the mid to late nineteenth century, characters from literature were joined by cavaliers, roundheads and groups at the court of Charles II. Although this kind of painting led to flights of ineffable vulgarity, it is well to be reminded that it was paralleled in France and Italy by painters of the Meissonier stamp like François Brunery, Georges Croegaert and Adolphe Lesrel; even Paul Delaroche exhibited *Cromwell looking at the Dead Body of Charles I* at the Royal Academy in 1850. At its worst this style of painting degenerated into the 'Cardinals tippling' variety which pandered to the meanest tastes on both sides of the Channel. To the uneducated patron historical accuracy was of little account.

Above left:
EDWARD MATTHEW WARD, R.A. *The Novel Reader.* $8\frac{1}{4} \times 9\frac{1}{2}$ inches. Exhibited at the Royal Academy in 1851. Signed on the reverse. Private collection, Great Britain.

Above right:
FRANK STONE, A.R.A. *The Sisters.* $20\frac{1}{4} \times 16$ inches. Signed. A. Class, Esq.

Below left:
WILLIAM HENRY HUNT. *Girl asleep in a Chair.* Water-colour. $12 \times 9\frac{3}{4}$ inches. Maas Gallery, London.

Les Femmes Savantes by C. R. Leslie is reproduced in colour on p. 120.

C. R. Leslie, the biographer of Constable, was one of the first to practise historical genre painting successfully. He was born in London of American parents, and brought up in Philadelphia. Coming to England he was patronised by Lord Egremont and, like Turner, stayed frequently at Petworth. A love of Hogarth and the theatre is discernible in his pictures. He could be delightfully brash, as in *Les Femmes Savantes*, or low-keyed as in *Le Bourgeois Gentilhomme*, both depicting

Below right:
WILLIAM GUSH. *Portraits of Rhoda and Sophie Baird.* $30 \times 25\frac{1}{2}$ inches. Sir Arthur Elton, Bt.
Painted in 1851. Rhoda (1834-1913) and Sophie (1836-1874) Baird were daughters of Rhoda Baird who later married Sir Arthur Hallam Elton.

scenes from Molière. Pictures of this kind were also rooted in the Boydell tradition of Shakespearian illustration. Henry Perronet Briggs (?1791–1844) painted Shakespearian scenes which link this tradition with Leslie.

Of the members of The Clique, Richard Dadd, Augustus Egg, John Phillip, W. P. Frith and H. N. O'Neil, it was Frith who achieved the widest fame. Egg was later to be affected by the Pre-Raphaelite movement; that he was already a painter capable of a smooth finish is apparent from *Scene from the Winter's Tale*, exhibited in 1845. If Dadd is to us the most interesting of this group, Frith, who was born in the same year as the Queen and lived to within a few months of the accession of George V, gained the most worldly success. Like Watts, he lived to be derided by the new aesthetes and branded as a bourgeois reactionary. He was regarded as a particularly virulent specimen of Victorian philistinism. His highly entertaining memoirs, written when he was over seventy, while they give us vivid glimpses of the Victorian artistic scene, contain many examples of almost ingenuous opportunism which strengthened this atti-

CHARLES BAXTER. *The Sisters.*
Diameter 12¾ inches. Victoria and
Albert Museum, London.

later period are examples of his Pre-Raphaelite stamina, the brilliantly conceived *Lady of Shalott* and the serenely beautiful *May Morning on Magdalen Tower*, for which, characteristically, he mounted the tower roof for several weeks 'about four in the morning with my small canvas to watch for the first rays of the rising sun'. These splendid anachronisms were painted when Whistler's *Nocturnes* were already a memory.

Ford Madox Brown remained the most formidable of the associates. Two of his pictures, *The Last of England* and *Work*, both started in 1852 and painted with true Pre-Raphaelite patience and discipline, are outstanding. In particular, *The Last of England* is one of the most poignant symbols of the Victorian scene and, like *Work*, it treats a contemporary theme. The first is a commentary on the emigration movement of the 'fifties and the departure of Woolner for the Australian goldfields, and the other reflects his admiration for the ideas of Carlyle and F. D. Maurice, in whose Working Men's College he taught for two years. Like William Morris, for whose firm he worked in the 'sixties, Brown was always concerned with social problems. His pictures are often encumbered by long

glosses, but he nevertheless intended them to be easily understood. Of his *Pretty Baa Lambs* he stressed that there was no 'meaning beyond the obvious one . . .

This picture was painted out in the sunlight; the only intention being to render that effect as well as my powers in a first attempt of that kind would allow.' Indeed his small out-door scenes of the 'fifties, for which he used a white ground, since there 'is nothing like a good coating of white to get a bright sunny colour', are a vital vindication of Pre-Raphaelite landscape painting, *Walton-on-the-Naze* and *An English Autumn Afternoon* (both at Birmingham), ranking high as examples. Brown never achieved the same degree of worldly success as some other Pre-Raphaelite painters, and later returned to his earlier subject-matter of history and romantic literature, painted in the flatulent baroque manner he had acquired in Belgium under Baron Wappers.

While Rossetti, balanced uneasily between poetry and painting, was groping about the dimly lit world of Dante and Beatrice, 'with the ambiguous light', as Max Beerbohm said, 'of a red torch somewhere in a dense fog', the bright star of Pre-Raphaelitism had become a constellation. If Rossetti was only interested in the social side of Pre-Raphaelitism, to others it was an opportunity, however momentary, to invest their dreams with a burning reality. The luminaries of this second order included some such as William Windus

(1822–1907) and John Brett (1830–1902) who were, in different ways, dimmed by the vehement proselytizing of Ruskin; others, including Henry Wallis (1830–1916), painter of *The Death of Chatterton* (Tate Gallery), and William Shakespeare Burton (1824–1916), painter of *The Wounded Cavalier*, demonstrated that they each only had sufficient afflatus for one Pre-Raphaelite masterpiece, although Wallis's *The Stone-breaker* (Birmingham), as an essay in social realism, comes close in quality. Walter Deverell (1827–1854) was more promising, but *The Pet* (Tate Gallery) remains his only well-known picture; similarly Henry Alexander Bowler (1824–1903) is remembered only for *The Doubt: 'Can these dry Bones live?'* (Tate Gallery); while *Jerusalem and the Valley of Jehoshaphat* is almost the sole monument to the memory of Thomas Seddon (1821–1856). Others such as Augustus Egg (1816–1863), William Dyce and James Smetham (1821–1889) were blown off course in mid-career, albeit achieving a heightened degree of intensity in their paintings, as in Egg's series *Past and Present* (Tate Gallery), and Dyce's *George Herbert at Bemerton*, *Gethsemane* and, one of the greatest of all Victorian paintings, *Pegwell Bay*.

Windus was the first provincial Pre-Raphaelite. He was a Liverpool artist, and his enthusiasm on seeing

ARTHUR HUGHES. *Bed-Time*. 40×52 inches. Harris Art Gallery, Preston.

Exhibited at the Royal Academy in 1862. The painting depicts an honest yeoman having returned from work, while his wife supervises bed-time prayers. 'The Art Journal' of 1862 commented on its 'dull solemnity' and 'cheerless piety'.

The Wounded Cavalier by W. S. Burton is reproduced in colour on p. 156.

Opposite page, below:
FORD MADOX BROWN. *The Traveller*. Panel. 12¼×18 inches. Signed with monogram and dated '84. City Art Galleries, Manchester.

The subject of this picture, which was begun in 1868 and finished in 1884, is said to have been taken from a poem by Victor Hugo. There is a water-colour version, dated 1868, at the Fitzwilliam Museum, Cambridge.

HENRY WALLIS. *Chatterton*. 24½ ×36¾ inches, arched top. Signed and dated 1856. Tate Gallery, London.

Exhibited at the Royal Academy in 1856. Popularly known as *The Death of Chatterton*, it was painted in the attic at Gray's Inn where the despairing young poet died by poisoning himself. George Meredith was the model, and two years later the artist eloped with Meredith's wife, who was the daughter of Thomas Love Peacock.

Millais's *Carpenter's Shop* at the Royal Academy in 1850 led to the Liverpool Academy becoming an important centre for Pre-Raphaelite painting. *Too Late* is his best known picture; *Burd Helen*, exhibited three years previously, was his first attempt in the new manner. Ruskin delivered a vicious attack on *Too Late*, 'Something wrong here; either the painter has been ill, or his picture has been sent to the Academy in a hurry . . . in time you may be a painter. Not otherwise.' The effect of this on the artist's neurotic temperament, together with his wife's death, was to cause him virtually to cease production and to make a bonfire of his works twenty-seven years before his death. Brett's failing was to follow too closely the precepts of Ruskin. After one undisputed masterpiece, *The Stone-breaker*, and other works of a high order such as *The Val d'Aosta* and *Glacier of Rosenlaui*, he painted a large number of monotonously geological coastal scenes and seascapes, only occasionally rising above mediocrity.

ARTHUR HUGHES. *Ophelia*. 27 ×48¾ inches. Signed. City Art Galleries, Manchester.

Exhibited at the Royal Academy in 1852. This is Hughes's first important picture, and was exhibited in the same year as Millais's *Ophelia*, although both artists were unaware, until varnishing day, that they had painted pictures identical in subject matter.

April Love by Arthur Hughes is reproduced in colour on p. 140.

AUGUSTUS EGG, R.A. *Past and Present, Number 3.* 25×30 inches. Signed and dated 1858. Tate Gallery, London.

Exhibited at the Royal Academy in 1858. This is the third of a series of three paintings showing the dire consequences of a wife's infidelity. The scene is a bridge near the Strand.

The position of Arthur Hughes (1830–1915) amongst the Pre-Raphaelites was like that of Keats among the Romantic poets. The tremulous lyricism of pictures like *April Love*, *The Tryst*, *The Long Engagement*, *Home from Sea* and *The Nativity*, painted as they are in soft glowing colours, with a sensitivity and sweetness bordering on pain, makes them a pictorial Victorian equivalent of the Odes. Hughes had once studied under Alfred Stevens, and it was not until 1850, through reading 'The Germ', that he made contact with the Pre-Raphaelites. Millais was to have the strongest influence over him, and his work deteriorated, as Millais's did. In contrast to Millais, however, Hughes's

paintings lost their public favour; and he fumbled about on the edge of Fairyland, although he never painted a satisfactory fairy picture. Some of his genius persisted in book illustration. *Bed-time*, exhibited at the Royal Academy in 1862, illustrates the direction his powers as a social commentator might have taken him.

Pre-Raphaelitism took a decisive new turn in 1856, when Rossetti met Edward Burne-Jones (1833–1898), who with William Morris (1834–1896), was an undergraduate at Oxford. At last Rossetti was able to exert the strongest influence of any of the original Brotherhood. Temperamentally unsuited to the rigours of hard-edge Pre-Raphaelitism, Rossetti had painted a

WILLIAM DYCE, R.A. *George Herbert at Bemerton*. 34 × 44 inches. Guildhall Art Gallery, London.

Exhibited at the Royal Academy in 1861. George Herbert (1593–1633), the poet and divine, was Vicar of Bemerton, near Salisbury; the Cathedral spire can be seen in the background. A reviewer in 'The 'Art Journal' wrote of this picture: 'if these trees, and ivy leaves, and grass, and wild flowers, be all painted in oils from nature, without the aid of photography or watercolours, then must this picture be considered . . . a marvellous triumph of manipulative success and skill'.

number of pictures symbolizing aspects of ideal love, which, reflecting his own experiences, were weighted with fatalism. He had recently painted *Paolo and Francesca* and *Dante's Dream at the Time of the Death of Beatrice* and *Dantis Amor* (his one realistic work in contemporary dress, *Found*, was left unfinished at the time of his death), but now multiple figure compositions were giving way to single idealized portraits. The love, anguish and remorse following the death of Elizabeth Siddal after a long illness and an overdose of laudanum prompted a series beginning with *Beata Beatrix* (1863), of which he did six replicas. These were followed by portraits of Fanny Cornforth, Alice Wilding, Jane Morris and others, in which the Rossetti type of the ideal woman was created. Redolent of poetry, these luscious visions of long-necked women with backgrounds of intricately curving and twisting plant forms, and their mythological titles such as *Pandora*, *Proserpine* and *Mnemosyne* were to establish, with the aid of Burne-Jones and Morris, the basis of what one might call the mythographic school. The artists who were associated with this late flowering of the Movement, Simeon Solomon (1840–1905), Frederick Sandys (1829–1904), Walter Crane (1845–1915), Frederic Shields (1833–1911) and ultimately Aubrey Beardsley (1872–1898), all played variations on this mythographic ideal. Albert Moore (1841–1893) who matured in a Pre-Raphaelite *milieu*, brought something of its flavour to Neo-classicism, rendering exquisite colour effects from the harmonious arrangement of flesh and drapery: thus was Whistler, who

ARTHUR HUGHES. *Home from Sea.* Panel. 20 × 25¾ inches. Signed and dated 1863. Ashmolean Museum, Oxford.

This picture is characteristic of Hughes's early and best manner.

Right:
JOHN BRETT, A.R.A. *Glacier at Rosenlaui.* 17½ × 16½ inches. Signed and dated Aug. 23/56. Tate Gallery, London.

Exhibited at the Royal Academy in 1857. This picture, which clearly shows the influence of Ruskin, was the first landscape Brett exhibited.

Left:
WILLIAM DYCE, R.A. *Gethsemane.* 16½ × 12⅜ inches. Walker Art Gallery, Liverpool.

Painted in about 1850.

was indebted to Moore, affected by the Rossetti prototype.

Shortly after his meeting with Rossetti, Burne-Jones emerged as an artist in his own right, and when Morris founded his firm, Morris, Marshall, Faulkner & Co., in 1861, with Rossetti, Madox Brown and Burne-Jones as co-directors, Burne-Jones was obliged to furnish an unending supply of decorative figures. He had already, in 1857, made cartoons for stained glass, and he was expected to work in this medium and even in tapestry design. An early familiarity with Malory's 'Le Morte D'Arthur', coupled with the poetic exploration of Northern myth by Morris in 'The Defence of Guenevere' and 'The Earthly Paradise', was to prove

a fertile source of subject-matter. Three visits to Italy, the second with Ruskin in 1862, taught him much about Italian art, and friendship with Leighton, Watts and his future brother-in-law Poynter helped him to overcome technical difficulties. It was the coupling of the 'Rossetti type' with his most abiding love, Arthurian romance, which laid the foundations of his creative life. He forged a bond between the idealistic latin temperament of Rossetti and the ideologically realistic nordic temperament of Morris, fusing the style of one with the mythology of the other. A third factor, of immediate international, or, more specifically, French origin, was to form an apex. This was the Aesthetic movement, an apparently vague but nonetheless real

JOHN BRETT, A.R.A. *The Stonebreaker.* 19½ × 26⅞ inches. Signed and dated 1857-8. Walker Art Gallery, Liverpool.

Exhibited at the Royal Academy in 1858. Painted in Surrey, with Box Hill in the distance. The geological precision delighted Ruskin who wrote in his Academy Notes 'it goes beyond anything the Pre-Raphaelites have done yet . . . it is a marvellous picture, and may be examined inch by inch with delight'.

cult which had its origins in the doctrine of *L'Art pour L'Art*, formulated in the daring works of Gautier and Baudelaire, and later, in England, reflected by the writings of Walter Pater. Its main tenet was that art was independent of morality, and was self-sufficient in its ends. This was a concept utterly opposed to the Victorian insistence on moral content in painting, yet, with Whistler (although he had no time for those who posed as aesthetes) for a while at its head, the movement took root in England. At first, it was in a sense amoral, but after the publication of Baudelaire's 'Les Fleurs du Mal' in 1857, it began to take a decadent turn, maintaining an attitude in opposition to morality. The poetry of Swinburne and Dowson, the writings of Oscar Wilde and the work of Aubrey Beardsley are all more or less permeated with this new influence.

The new movement became merged with the Rossetti type of Pre-Raphaelitism, and Burne-Jones

SIR JOHN EVERETT MILLAIS, Bt., P.R.A. *Mariana*. Panel. 23½ × 19½ inches. Signed and dated 1851. The Rt Hon. Lord Sherfield G.C.B., G.C.M.G.

Exhibited at the Royal Academy in 1851. The picture was inspired by the following lines from Tennyson's poem 'Mariana':
'She only said, "My life is dreary, / He cometh not," she said; / She said, "I am aweary, aweary, / I would that I were dead!"'.
The stained glass was painted from windows in Merton College, Oxford; the garden seen through it was painted from that of his friend, Thomas Combe, at Oxford. The picture was poorly received at the Academy Exhibition. Ruskin, in his letter to 'The Times' on 13 May approved of it, but said he was glad to see that Millais's 'lady in blue is heartily tired of painted windows and idolatrous toilet table'. *See p. 127.*

Opposite page, right:
SIR EDWARD COLEY BURNE-JONES, Bt. *Sidonia von Bork, 1560.* Water-colour, 13 × 6¾ inches. Signed and dated 1860. Tate Gallery, London.

This water-colour and its companion, *Clara von Bork,* clearly reveal the influence of Rossetti, which pervaded Burne-Jones's early work. Sidonia von Bork was a character in 'Sidonia the Sorceress' by the Swiss writer Wilhelm Meinhold, which had aroused the enthusiasm of Rossetti. An English translation of the book by Jane Francisca, Lady Wilde (Oscar Wilde's mother), under the pseudonym 'Speranza', was published in 1893 by the Kelmscott Press.

Opposite page, left:
DANTE GABRIEL ROSSETTI. *Beata Beatrix.* 33¾ × 26½ inches. Signed with monogram and dated 1872. Predella. 9½ × 26½ inches. The Art Institute of Chicago.

This is one of six replicas Rossetti made of the original version, now at the Tate Gallery, which was painted in 1869, a year after the death of his wife, Elizabeth Siddal. Rossetti appended a lengthy gloss on the picture which illustrates the 'Vita Nuova', embodying symbolically the death of Beatrice as treated in that work. The artist gave his wife's features to Beatrice. The Chicago version has a predella showing the meeting of Dante and Beatrice in Paradise. The original frame is characteristic of the type evolved by Rossetti, and often associated with Pre-Raphaelite pictures.

became the torch-bearer. When Burne-Jones said that he meant by a picture 'a beautiful romantic dream of something that never was, never will be—in a light better than any light that ever shone—in a land no one can define or remember, only desire' he was in effect adhering to the new trends of Aestheticism.

SIR EDWARD COLEY BURNE-JONES, Bt. *Study for Part of the Arras Tapestry made by Morris and Co. for Mr D'Arcy of Stanmore Hall, Middlesex, depicting the Quest for the Holy Grail.* Water-colour and body-colour. $11\frac{1}{4} \times 26\frac{1}{2}$ inches. Mr and Mrs Richard Moore.

Painted in about 1893. The shields are those of King Arthur's knights.

Opposite page, left:
ARTHUR HUGHES. *April Love.* $35 \times 19\frac{1}{2}$ inches. Tate Gallery, London.

Exhibited at the Royal Academy in 1856. The picture was inspired by the following lines from Tennyson's 'Miller's Daughter': 'Love is hurt with jar and fret. / Love is made a vague regret. / Eyes with idle tears are wet. / Idle habit links us yet. / What is love? For we forget: / Ah, no! no!'
The picture was bought by William Morris, then an undergraduate at Oxford, at the Academy exhibition, to the disappointment of Ruskin who had tried to persuade his father to buy it. 'Exquisite in every way', Ruskin wrote in his Academy Notes, 'lovely in colour, most subtle in the quivering expression of the lips, and sweetness of the tender face, shaken, like a leaf by winds upon its dew, and hesitating back into peace'. A study in oils is in the possession of Mr John Gere. *See p. 135.*

Opposite page, above right:
JAMES COLLINSON. *The Empty Purse.* $24 \times 19\frac{3}{8}$ inches. Tate Gallery, London.

Painted in about 1857. Of the three versions of this picture, this is probably the last to be painted. The other versions are at Sheffield City Art Galleries and Nottingham Art Gallery.

Opposite page, below right:
DANTE GABRIEL ROSSETTI. *The Wedding of St. George and Princess Sabra.* Water-colour. $13\frac{1}{2} \times 13\frac{1}{2}$ inches. Signed with monogram and dated 1857. Tate Gallery, London.

In 1857 Rossetti was closely associated with William Morris. A year later Rossetti wrote to the American Charles Eliot Norton: 'these chivalric, Froissartian themes are quite a passion of mine'.

DANTE GABRIEL ROSSETTI. *The Wedding of Saint George.* Water-colour and body-colour. $11 \times 13\frac{1}{2}$ inches. Signed with monogram, inscribed and dated 1864. Dr Jerrold N. Moore.

The composition of this picture was originally conceived as the last of a series of six stained glass windows illustrating the story of St. George and the Dragon, designed for Morris, Marshall, Faulkner and Co in 1861/2. There is a pencil study, drawn in 1857, at Birmingham.

WALTER CRANE. *Ormuzd and Ahrimanes*. Water-colour and body-colour. $10\frac{3}{4} \times 29\frac{3}{4}$ inches. Signed with monogram and dated 1868-70. Charles Jerdein, Esq.

Crane wrote of this, his first allegorical composition, that it was 'an endeavour to suggest the Parsi idea of the struggle of the spirits of good and evil through the ages. The design showed two armed knights fighting on horseback, one white and the other black, by the side of a river winding away in long serpentine curves, showing at each bend some typical relic of time in the shape of a temple of some lost faith —here an Egyptian gateway, there a Celtic dolmen, a classic temple and a Gothic cathedral—the whole effect being of a subdued twilight, as of the dawn'.

Below right:
ELIZABETH SIDDAL. *The Lady of Shalott*. Pen and ink. $7\frac{3}{4} \times 9\frac{3}{4}$ inches. Signed and dated Dec 15, '53. Maas Gallery, London.

The drawing illustrates Tennyson's poem.

Below left:
DANTE GABRIEL ROSSETTI. *Elizabeth Siddal*. Pen and ink. $6\frac{1}{2} \times 3\frac{1}{2}$ inches. Cecil Higgins Museum, Bedford.

Inscribed on the reverse in W. M. Rossetti's hand: 'Liz 1855 as late as '58.'

Burne-Jones's pictures, with their limpid rhythms scarcely seen in English painting since Romney, their wan, 'sublimely sexless' figures moving silently about the half-lit world of ancient legend depicted with finely-graded spatial and colour harmonies, are as entirely free of didactic or moral purpose as the paintings of Whistler, whom Burne-Jones knew well in the 'sixties. After 'seven blissfullest years [with] no publicity, no exhibiting, no getting pictures done against time', he suddenly acquired celebrity with the exhibition of seven of his pictures at the Grosvenor Gallery in 1877. To Henry James, who saw the exhibition, Burne-Jones stood 'quite at the head of English painters of our day'. These pictures included *The Days of Creation*, *The Mirror of Venus* and *The Beguiling of Merlin*. 'It is,' wrote James, 'the Art of culture, of reflection, of intellectual luxury, of aesthetic refinement, of people who look at the world and at life not

Above:
SIMEON SOLOMON. '*And the sons of God saw the daughters of men that they were fair*'. Water-colour and body-colour. $10\frac{3}{4} \times 7\frac{1}{4}$ inches. Signed with monogram and dated 11.63. Private collection, London.

The subject is taken from Genesis, VI.ii.

Right:
DANTE GABRIEL ROSSETTI. *Astarte Syriaca*. 72×42 inches. Signed and dated 1877. City Art Galleries, Manchester.

The principal figure represents Mrs William Morris (Jane Burden), although she did not sit for the painting. Rossetti describes the painting in his sonnet 'Mystery; lo! betwixt the sun and moon . . .' David Roberts, writing to James Nasmyth (1808-1890) in 1864, the last year of his life, made a despairing comment on the perplexities of Pre-Raphaelitism, of which this picture may be regarded as the embodiment '. . . I rub my eyes to find whether I am in a dream. This new phase of art may after all have its charms for the rising generation, though unseen by me; but they as well as I must come to the same conclusion, that if this be right, then all that has been done before is wrong'.

directly, as it were, and in all its accidental reality, but in the reflection and ornamental portrait of it furnished by art itself in other manifestations; furnished by literature, by poetry, by history, by erudition.'

Burne-Jones's pictorial work, in which there was a decreasing distinction between media (Ruskin once declared in Burne-Jones's studio that 'every one of

143

these works is in pure water-colour', when in fact all of them were in oils) ranged from the early exercises like *The Flower of God*, *The Madness of Sir Tristram*, and *Fair Rosamond*, which was owned by Ruskin, to large oil paintings, such as *Laus Veneris*, *The Wheel of Fortune*, *The Golden Stairs* and *Love and the Pilgrim*, many of which occupied him over a number of years. In some of his later work the dramatic element is so reduced that the pictures border on abstraction. Robin Ironside (*Horizon*, I; 1940) suggested that, had Burne-Jones's reputation not been submerged by New English Impressionism, the British would have been better equipped to accept the modern movement. As it was, in the 'eighties he was a figure of international importance, first in France, and later in Spain and Germany.

This second wave of Pre-Raphaelitism produced not so much a constellation as a diffuse cluster, less intensified, more vitiated and touched by more influences than the first group. The example of 'Truth to Nature' was followed by many genre and landscape painters; these are the true descendants of the Brotherhood, but many of them worked in a vacuum, cheated of their birthright, like poor relations. A few derived their style more or less directly from Rossetti and ran a somewhat erratic course parallel to that of Burne-Jones: Frederick Sandys, one of the most successful of Pre-Raphaelite portraitists, a painter of mythological subjects, and a

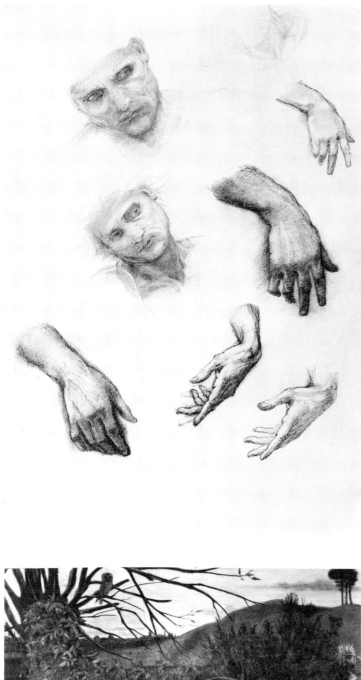

WILLIAM MULREADY, R.A. *Bathers*. Black and red chalks. 43 × 55 inches. National Gallery of Scotland, Edinburgh. Drawn about 1849.

rarely equalled in nineteenth century English painting. Thackeray praised him for painting 'in the grandest and broadest style . . . Look for a while at Mr Etty's pictures, and away you rush, your "eyes on fire", drunken with the luscious colours that are poured out for you on the liberal canvas, and warm with the sight of the beautiful sirens that appear on it.' Etty was elected a Royal Academician in 1828. He returned to York in 1848, a famous man, to die there a year later. His funeral was attended by large numbers of civic dignitaries, citizens, relatives and friends. Etty was a powerful and original artist, but he cannot be placed in the very front rank. In spite of their naturalness, many of his figures are marred by careless anatomical drawing, and he never finally succeeded in making convincing finished pictures from his sketches; to balance these defects he has a richness and vigour in his colouring which often invites comparison with Delacroix.

Etty's influence was pervasive. Among those who fell under his spell were Edward Calvert and John Phillip. Even Orchardson's early work contains echoes of Etty. Millais, in his student days, was a keen follower of Etty, and was to reaffirm in later years his admir-

167

SIR LAWRENCE ALMA-TADEMA, O.M., R.A. *In the Tepidarium*. Panel. 9½ × 13 inches. Signed with Opus no. CCXXIX. Lady Lever Art Gallery, Port Sunlight.

Painted in 1881 and exhibited at the Grosvenor Gallery in 1883.

Opposite page, left:
EDWARD CALVERT. *Semi-draped figures*. Prepared paper. 12½ × 7¼ inches. Walter Brandt, Esq.

ation for him. G. F. Watts, although more of the gloomy moralist, and no less pious than Etty, owed the older artist a profound debt which affected his work all his life. William Frost was an early protégé. His work is largely a pallid reflection of Etty's style; but at its best it bears a distinctive charm, with its pearly-tinted Victorian nudes. Alfred Woolmer (1805–1892) translated Etty's subject-matter into Watteauesque settings.

William Mulready took up nude painting rather late in life. His *Women Bathing* was exhibited at the Royal Academy in 1849; in the same year he painted *The Bathers*. His biographer F. G. Stephens regretted that 'he wilfully reduced the extremities of the nudities till they were out of proportion to the rest of the figures'. Stephens also applied these strictures to the so-called 'Academy Studies', which Mulready began drawing in 1840, at the suggestion of his son, Michael. They are, nevertheless, perfect models of academic drawing, generally superior to those of Alfred Elmore.

In academic drawing, pride of place is surely held by Alfred Stevens (1817–1875), the sculptor and decorative artist. He was born in Blandford, the son of a carpenter, decorator and sign painter, and kindly friends arranged for him to study in Italy. Often near starvation he copied frescoes in Florence and the works of Andrea del Sarto in Naples, and sketched at Pompeii, paying his way by selling his drawings. In Rome he studied under Thorwaldsen. When he returned he was fully confident of his very considerable powers in painting, drawing, carving, sculpture and design. Stevens's life was spoilt by bad luck and lack of real recognition; bureaucratic controversy condemned him during his last eighteen years to spasmodic work on the Wellington monument. The sheets of figure studies from which he worked are remarkable for their extraordinary vigour and assurance; not until the early drawings of Augustus John (1878–1961) do we find such clear, incisive, yet fluent line; moreover, the female nudes in his less academic studies project overtones of healthy sexuality, which anticipate those of the younger artist.

From the 'sixties until the age of Beardsley, Conder, early Steer and Sickert, nude painting was mainly

confined to Burne-Jones and his disciples; and the neo-classical painters were able to paint nudes freely by placing them in varying degrees of deshabille in the *tepidarium*, *frigidarium* or *apodyterium*. Many of the most illustrious painters, like Millais and Frith, completely ignored the nude, except in their student days. And with nudes painted by Burne-Jones and Albert Moore, one is often scarcely aware that the figures are nude at all, so completely are they subordinated to the central idea of design on the rarefied plane of High Art. Steer's nudes suffer by usually being compounded of Watteau, Rubens or Boucher, although he was capable of fine work; no less derivative, Conder's nudes are beautiful generalities basking in a silken twilight, with a kind of insubstantial eroticism. It was left to Aubrey Beardsley to be the first to elevate the nude to its most erotic level, particularly in the *Lysistrata* series, but so exquisite is the style, so refined the technique, that

Above right:
PHILIP WILSON STEER. *The Toilet of Venus.* 34×44 inches. Williamson Art Gallery and

Museum, Birkenhead.
This study was painted in about 1898. The finished picture is at the Tate Gallery.

Below right:
CHARLES CONDER. *The Bathers.* 28×36 inches. Mr Robert T. Hamlin, Jr.

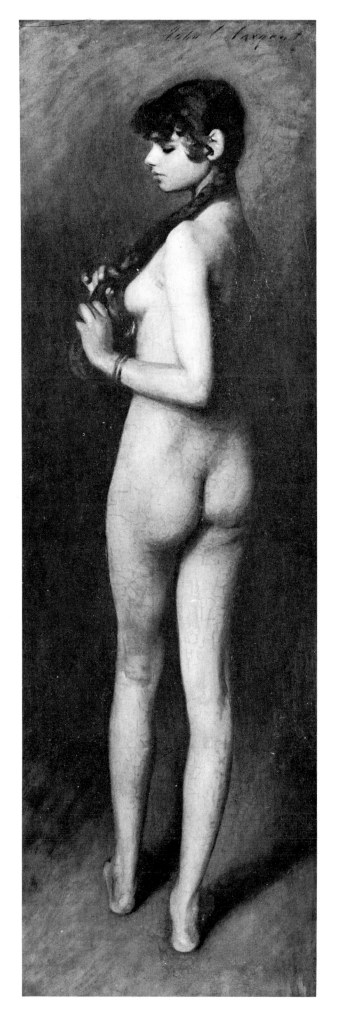

JAMES McNEILL WHISTLER.
Venus Astarte. Chalk and pastel.
10 $\frac{3}{16}$ × 7$\frac{1}{4}$ inches. Signed with
butterfly device. Freer Gallery of
Art, Washington.
  Drawn in the late 'nineties.

his nudes cause less offence than some of the embarrassingly naked goddesses that adorned the walls of the Royal Academy exhibitions of the time. It seems a pity that Whistler should not have painted more nudes: in the late 'nineties he painted and drew a number, which, had he attempted to do so earlier, might have rivalled those of Degas; and in *Venus Astarte*, the essence of classical beauty is achieved.

John Singer Sargent (1856–1925) rarely attempted naturalistic nude painting in his early years, but his fondness for dusky exotic beauty resulted in at least one suave essay in sophistication, *The Egyptian Girl*. With the lovely nudes of Ethel Walker (1861–1951), the bathing men and boys of H. S. Tuke, the 'back-bedroom' subjects of Sickert and the lively studies of Augustus John, nude painting was continued into the twentieth century.

The interest in still-life painting grew in response to the increasing materialism of the wealthy middle classes, and, of course, to the pleas of Ruskin for painters to pursue the earnest study of nature. With the exception of William Etty, William Henry Hunt (1790–1864) and others of the 'bird's-nest' school, still-life painting was dominated by the East Anglians. Etty strayed into the territory of still-life very late—in September 1839, to be exact—at a time when it might have been supposed that he had no surprises left to spring. Although still-lifes comprise a small fraction of his work, and are inevitably in the Dutch tradition, the painting is spirited and accurate. The very few still-life paintings done by William Müller suggest the

example of Van Huysum. Peter De Wint, as one might expect, considering his Dutch ancestry, painted some of the finest still-lifes in water-colour by any artist of the English School. For a painter whose landscapes are characterized by broad effects, his ability to evoke tactile values is remarkable.

William Henry Hunt, the son of a tin-plate worker, was once the pupil of John Varley, as were Copley Fielding, Linnell and Mulready. He and Linnell formed a close friendship, and between 1805 and 1809 they occupied themselves with sketching tours on the River Thames, as Thomas Girtin and Turner had done before them. By 1807 he was exhibiting at the Royal

PHILIP WILSON STEER. *Seated Nude: The Black Hat.* 20 × 16 inches. Signed. Tate Gallery, London.
Painted in about 1900.

Left:
ALFRED STEVENS. *Girl with a Topknot.* Red crayon and pencil. 14⅝ × 10⅞ inches. Walker Art Gallery, Liverpool.

Opposite page, right:
JOHN SINGER SARGENT, R.A. *Egyptian Girl.* 73 × 23 inches. Signed. Roger McCormick.
Painted in Egypt in 1891.

Academy, and, after a period with Dr Monro, he was patronized by the Earl of Essex. By the 'twenties Hunt was already proficient at painting lovely figure subjects and still-life pictures, becoming famous for his

WILLIAM HENRY HUNT *Grapes and Pomegranates*. Water-colour. $7\frac{1}{2} \times 11$ inches. Signed. Mr and Mrs Cyril Fry.

Above right:
WILLIAM CRUIKSHANK. *Still Life with Bird, Bird's Nest and Blossom.* Water-colour and body-colour. Oval. 7×9 inches. Signed. Fine Art Society, Ltd., London.

WILLIAM ETTY, R.A. *Still Life with Glass.* Panel. $12\frac{1}{2} \times 16\frac{1}{4}$ inches. Henry E. Huntington Library and Art Gallery, U.S.A.

Exhibited at the Royal Scottish Academy in 1843, where it was entitled *A Study of Fruit*.

bird's-nest subjects. These earned him the soubriquet 'Bird's-nest' Hunt. Painted in rich water-colour and delicately stippled, these studies, of which nearly eight hundred were shown over the years at the Society of Painters in Water-Colours, became greatly loved by Victorians. 'If I were the Duke of Devonshire,' Thackeray sighed, 'I would have a couple of Hunts in every room in all my houses.' Ruskin commended him for having 'defied all false teaching', hung one in his bedroom at Brantwood, and compared him to 'the best Dutch Masters'. Hunt fathered a large litter of imitators, who at their best came close to rivalling him. These included William Cruikshank, who exhibited at the Royal Academy, William Hough (exhib. 1857–

1894), John Sherrin (1819–1896), and two brothers, George and Oliver Clare. A painting family called Coleman specialized in still-life and flower subjects: of these, the best was Helen Cordelia (1847–1884) who achieved real distinction in her studies of nature. William Hughes (1842–1901), who usually worked in oils, had an accurate eye for detail. These closely detailed studies of nature by Hunt and his followers provided the backcloth for fairy paintings.

Partly due, no doubt, to their traditional affinities with Holland, the most vigorous school of flower and still-life painters was of East Anglian origin. Norwich was the birth-place of two famous botanists, Sir Edward Smith, the founder of the Linnean Society in

PETER DE WINT. *Still Life.* Water-colour. 7×9 inches. J. L. F. Wright, Esq.

EDWARD LADELL. *Still Life.*
17 × 14 inches. R. Clement Wilson,
Esq.

Right:
WILLIAM JAMES MÜLLER.
Still-life. 30 × 25 inches. Fine Art
Society Ltd., London.

Fruit-piece by Eloise Harriet Stannard is reproduced in colour on
p. 160.

1788, and Sir William Hooker, one of the great directors of Kew Gardens. Of considerable merit and relatively cheap to buy, the works of the East Anglian painters found favour with the new collecting class. Amongst the school were several women of more than merely professional competence. Mrs Joseph Stannard (1803–1885), well known as Emily Coppin, had studied and copied Van Huysum in Holland; she and her daughter, Emily Stannard, were painters of some merit. Eloise Harriet Stannard (1829–1915), the daughter of Alfred Stannard (1806–1889) himself a landscape and marine painter, painted a large number of particularly luscious flower and still-life paintings: her ability to render the bloom of a plum or the trans-

lucency of a white currant is well conveyed in her circular painting of fruit. A comparable artist was Edward Ladell, a native of Colchester, who exhibited regularly at the Royal Academy between 1856 and 1885. George Lance (1802–1864), a pupil of Haydon, narrowly escaped the trap of historical painting by being discovered by Sir George Beaumont, who bought a still-life which he had painted to improve his technique. Other commissions followed, and soon he was painting still-life almost exclusively, with a sensitive feeling for texture and a rich, although occasionally rather too sharp, palette. His pupil William Duffield (1816–1863) was less lucky than his master: on the threshold of a promising career as a still-life painter, he frequently added dead game to the composition, and 'owed his last illness,' according to the Redgraves, 'to the earnest pursuit of his profession. He was painting a dead stag, which remained in his studio for that purpose until it became extremely decayed. Unfortunately the painter, from a prior illness, had lost his sense of smell' and in 'the presence of miasma, he continued to work unconscious of the danger, until the infection took place which caused his death.' Even still-life painting has its hazards. During the last years of the Victorian age, still-life painting found fewer practitioners: there were occasional exceptions, like Hercules Brabazon Brabazon (1821–1906), who was well able to paint an occasional brilliant flower-piece or still-life.

XII

NEO-CLASSICAL PAINTERS

In the second half of the nineteenth century, England had an opulent, powerful and expanding society, with ever-increasing responsibilities. Whatever religious doubts assailed intellectuals, the average middle and upper class Victorians had an unflinching faith in their country's destiny: they believed they were ruled by great statesmen, motivated by high and just ideals; they were secure in the thought that the most powerful navy in the world kept the *Pax Britannica*, and protected the trade-routes of the largest Empire the world had ever known. Its European neighbours may have

LORD LEIGHTON OF STRETTON, P.R.A. *Perseus and Andromeda*. 91 × 50 inches. Walker Art Gallery, Liverpool.

Exhibited at the Royal Academy in 1891. Leighton made figurines of Perseus mounted on Pegasus and of Andromeda. F. G. Stephens wrote

of this picture: '*Perseus and Andromeda* . . . has always seemed to me not only the aptest and best sustained version of the legend which art has given us [but] incomparably the most poetical, strong, and refined illustration of the subject from a dramatic point of view'.

been prone to political convulsions, but England was complacent in its well-ordered social system, and civic pride reflected the fundamental stability of Church and State. Even the propagation of liberal ideas was tolerated in a society so soundly constituted. The doctrine propounded by John Stuart Mill, of rebellion against the supine acceptance of conventional opinions, and the collision of Darwinism with religious belief, could be openly discussed only in a society certain of its own strength. This was a public more than ready to accept a kind of painting which mirrored its affluence, sturdiness and sense of justice, its power and its aspirations. And what better reflected its sublime self-assurance than the passion for the ancient civilizations of Greece and Rome?

Classical antiquity enjoyed great prestige. It had, of course, provided many of the themes of painting since the Renaissance; Flaxman's illustrations to

LORD LEIGHTON OF STRETTON, P.R.A. *Cimabue's celebrated Madonna is carried in Procession through the Streets of Florence . . .* 87¾ × 205 inches. Signed with monogram. Her Majesty the Queen.

Exhibited at the Royal Academy in 1855, when it was bought by Queen Victoria for £600. The title continues *. . . in front of the Madonna, and crowned with laurels, walks*

Cimabue himself, with his pupil Giotto; behind it, Arnolfo di Lapo, Gaddo Gaddi, Andrea Tafi, Nicola Pisano, Buffalmacco and Simone Memmi; in the corner, Dante. The picture was begun in the Spring of 1853 and completed in early 1855, in Rome. The design was made with the encouragement and advice of Steinle, and the picture was altered, when almost complete, at the

suggestion of Cornelius. Originally the procession moved straight from right to left; Leighton made it turn and face the spectator. The picture depicts the public glorification of art in early Florence, and reflects Leighton's own artistic idealism. The *Madonna* in Leighton's picture is now generally ascribed to Duccio.

Homer had had a European impact; the Elgin marbles, there for all to see, had been a constant stimulus; Haydon had seen in them 'principles which the common sense of English people would understand'. Antonio Canova, the great exponent of neo-classicism, had praised them highly. Indeed the principles of neo-classicism had been upheld successively by the sculptors Canova, Bertel Thorwaldsen and John Gibson until the death of Gibson in 1866. From mid-

century onwards its appeal was greatly enhanced by
archaeological discovery. 'The Last Days of Pompeii'
by Lord Lytton, published in 1834, soon became a
widely-read classic. The first fully systematic excava-
tions of Pompeii and Herculanaeum were carried out
in 1861 by the Italian government immediately after
the *Risorgimento*. The discovery of a civilization of
A.D. 79, buried since then under a thirty-foot layer of
volcanic ash, was swiftly made available to a fascinated public. 'What a display it is!' said Leighton, 'here
we are admitted into the most intimate privacy of a
multitude of Pompeian houses—the kitchens, the
pantries, the cellars of the contemporaries of the
Plinies have here no secret for us.' It soon became
apparent that Pompeian society was not all that different from Victorian society: there were indications
of a proletarian system on the move, of wealth based
on trade. All this was noted by another painter,
Lawrence Alma-Tadema (1836–1912), a Dutchman
who had settled in London in 1870.

The classical revival in painting had, however, taken
root earlier in England. By the nature of its subject
matter it was specially attractive to the academic
mentality. As a branch of High Art, it was not far
removed from historical painting: it was concerned
with lofty idealism and its themes were a subject of
scholarship. Although they were staunch upholders of
the traditions of the Royal Academy, it would be difficult to imagine Millais or Frith painting *Helen walking
on the Ramparts of Troy* or *Hercules wrestling with Death
for the Body of Alcestis*. Such themes required a wide
range of classical learning, an alert eye for new archaeological discovery and a painting technique to match
the subject.

These conditions were amply fulfilled by Frederic
Leighton (1830–1896). Leighton was born at Scarborough in Yorkshire. His father was an enlightened
doctor, something of the *homo universalis* which his son
was later to become. Leighton was encouraged by him
to acquire a thorough grounding in the Greek and
Latin classics. By the age of ten he was fully con-
versant with classical legend; by twelve he was fluent
in French and Italian, and a year or two later, in
German. Before he was twenty, he was widely travelled
in Europe, and deeply responsive to beauty in art,
architecture and music. At an early age he had shown
a strong inclination to become a painter. In the
enlightened and affluent style natural to his family he
was rushed through an intensive period of instruction
from the best continental teachers and academies.
After a short spell with the Roman drawing master,
Francesco Meli, he was admitted to the Florentine
Academy, where he studied under Bezzuoli and
Servolini, considered by the Italians as the Michel-
angelo and Raphael of their day. Leighton by no
means agreed with this evaluation. The quest for a

LORD LEIGHTON OF STRET-
TON, P.R.A. *Hercules Wrestling with
Death for the Body of Alcestis.* 52 × 104
inches. Charles Jerdein, Esq.
Exhibited at the Royal Academy
in 1871. Studies for this picture are
at Leighton House. Robert Brown-
ing paid a tribute to the picture and
its painter in 'Balaustion's Adven-
ture', published in the same year.

teacher who could match the exalted tenor of his mind
brought him finally to the last of the Nazarenes, and
the most uncompromisingly earnest of them all,
Edward Jacob von Steinle. On these foundations was
raised the great Olympian.

Leighton was handsome, sociable, fluent in many
languages, and possessed of a certain grandeur of
manner, which seemed already to mark him as one
predestined for high office. Thackeray, who met
Leighton in Rome, remarked to Millais when he
returned to London that he had met 'a versatile young
dog called Leighton, who will one of these days run
you hard' for the presidency of the Royal Academy.
Leighton's formative years were to have a profound
influence on English academic attitudes in the second
half of the century. A meeting with the neo-classical
sculptor, John Gibson, in Rome, the Germanic training of his intellect, and his spontaneous emotional
response to Italian art were all contributory to the
manner of his maturity. All that was needed now was
a large scale work to send to the Royal Academy: he
selected a subject, and accordingly began work on a
picture which he entitled *Cimabue's celebrated Madonna
is carried in Procession through the Streets of Florence.* It was
while he was engaged on this colossal picture that
there occurred one of those confrontations which constantly lent impetus to movements in Victorian

painting. Edward John Poynter (1836–1919) was in
Leighton's studio when the artist made a drastic
alteration to *Cimabue*, on the suggestion of Peter
Cornelius. Poynter promptly decided to paint grand
subjects with elevated themes and it was he who, with
Alma-Tadema, carried the style into the twentieth
century.

The exhibition of the picture in 1855, in the same
year as Millais's *The Rescue*, which was voted picture of
the year, was another of those decisive events which
marked the progress of English painting. It caused a
sensation. To William Blake Richmond (1842–1921),
then aged thirteen, 'it stood out among the other
pictures to my young eye as a work so complete, so
noble in design, so serious in sentiment and of such
achievement, that perforce it took me by the throat'.
Ruskin considered it 'a very important and very beautiful picture', but, crucially, and to Leighton's dismay,
he nevertheless thought Millais's picture was 'greater'
than *Cimabue*, because, as Leighton wrote to his mother,
'the joy of a mother over her rescued children is a
higher order of emotion than any expressed in my
picture'. *Cimabue* was, in fact, an early forerunner of
the cult of Aestheticism, of art for art's sake, of the
absence of moral content. Moreover, it was seized
upon by academic circles as the ideal counterweight
to Pre-Raphaelite heresies. As Rossetti wrote to

ception. Some, like Thomas Carrick (1802–1875), adopted the lucrative practice of colouring photographs, inspiring a contemporary critic to congratulate him for having given 'warmth and life, and expression to the cold, dead outline of the original photograph'; others like Sir William Newton, who in 1847 was a founder member of the first Photographic Club, embraced photography with enthusiasm. John Lavery recalled in his autobiography that he had served 'three years apprenticeship as a miniature painter over photographs on ivory'.

Similarly, the profusion of readily obtainable photographic references, the genre scenes popularized by the London Stereoscopic Company in about 1857, and the famous combination pictures by Rejlander and Robinson, all contributed to the decay of genre painting. The photographers pilfered remorselessly from the painters' subject matter, as some of their titles suggest: 'The Geography Lesson', 'The Spinning Wheel', 'Night Out—Homeless' and 'Feeding the Cat'. Some of these photographs achieved wide popularity, although they were considered rather vulgar by the critics. Their popularity grew and declined along with the paintings they emulated.

The effect of photography on landscape painting followed much the same insidious pattern, but the results were perhaps less far-reaching, except in one particular field. It severely curtailed the activities of foreign view painters: David Roberts and James Holland left no real successors. The camera had brought all the four corners of the world into the drawing room. Photographers like Francis Frith made

LONDON STEREOSCOPIC COMPANY. *Alfred, Lord Tennyson.* Radio Times Hulton Picture Library, London.
Taken in 1857-9. Julia Margaret Cameron made some memorable photographic portraits of Tennyson.

Below left:
GEORGE FREDERICK WATTS, O.M., R.A. *Alfred, Lord Tennyson.* 23½ × 19½ inches. National Portrait Gallery, London.
Painted in 1873. Watts painted seven portraits of Tennyson. 'What I try for,' Watts said while engaged on one of them, 'is the half-unconscious insistence upon the nobilities of the subject.'

LONDON STEREOSCOPIC COMPANY. *The Cat and the Goldfish.* Radio Times Hulton Picture Library, London.
Posed genre photograph taken c.1860.

201

journeys to Egypt, Palestine and Syria, and accurate records of architecture, mountains, archaeological and biblical sites came pouring back to England. Photography ensured once and for all the total collapse of the classical landscape tradition: the ordered assembly of form was simply incompatible with photography. A rhythm began to establish itself between painters and photographers: no sooner had the photographers borrowed subject-matter or effects from the painters than the style of painting which they copied declined in popularity. For instance, the popular moonlight scenes in the Pether tradition, which culminated in the effulgently atmospheric scenes by Atkinson Grimshaw, were closely paralleled by another Yorkshireman, a photographer called Frank Meadow Sutcliffe. Many of his photographic landscapes and scenes of Whitby Harbour contain the very essence of Grimshaw. Significantly, the moonlight tradition died with Grimshaw. This artist's landscapes are permeated with photographic vision, with their mists, the stencilling of branches or masts against a moonlit sky, the reflections of light on water, the dark smudgy figures which seem like shapes that have moved on a time-exposed photograph. Indeed, Grimshaw devised a technique whereby a master-drawing was thrown on to a canvas or board through a photographic enlarger, and by this method was able to paint several versions of the same subject. Antoine Claudet had perfected a process in

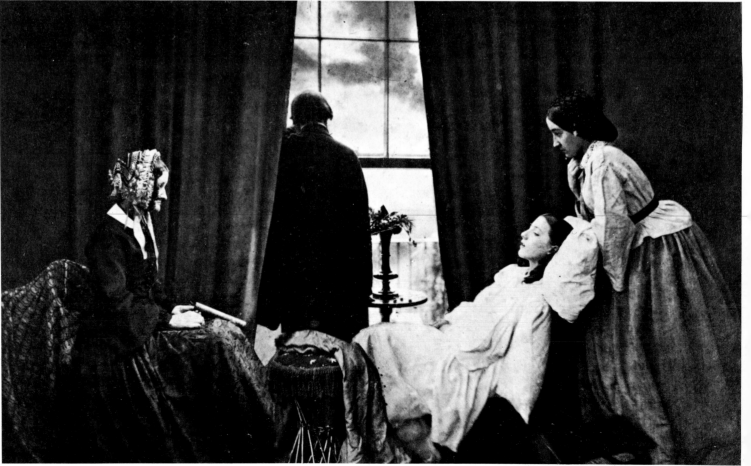

with a magic lantern; perhaps this was the method Grimshaw used. Although his paintings are quite valid as such, it would seem that photography and painting achieved their closest fusion in this artist, and the landscape tradition is none the poorer for the fact.

The art of still-life painting, never strong in England, almost certainly suffered at the hands of photographers. 'Photography,' as a writer in 'The Athenaeum' in January 1859 dared to hope, 'will in time

SIR LAWRENCE ALMA-TADEMA, O.M., R.A. *A Coign of Vantage*. Panel. $25\frac{1}{4} \times 17\frac{3}{4}$ inches. Signed with Opus no. CCCXXXIII and dated 1895. Mr Allen Funt.

Three Roman women watch the return of the galleys. The artist has created an illusion of great height and distance. *See p. 182.*

the 'sixties which he called 'Photosciagraphy', whereby a photographic image could be projected on a canvas

203

JOHN ATKINSON GRIMSHAW,
Liverpool Quay by Moonlight, 24 × 36
inches. Signed and dated 1887,
Tate Gallery, London.
When this picture was painted
Grimshaw had been living for the
better part of two years in Chelsea.
He also painted dockland scenes in
Glasgow and Greenock in the same
year. *See p. 229.*

entirely destroy all necessity of men wasting their time
in painting still-life.' Certainly the still-life painters
like Edward Ladell and George Lance left no successors of any importance, who could subsist almost
entirely on still-life painting. And while photographs
which used multiple-exposed and superimposed images
no doubt helped to encourage a fleeting credence in
supernatural and fairy paintings, the large numbers of
counterfeit spirit photographs surely hastened the
demise of fairy paintings.

Perhaps one of the most fruitful contributions of
photography to painting was in recording the appearance and movement of animals. In 1872, an English-
born photographer named Eadweard Muybridge,
who had emigrated to California, was consulted about
an old controversy—whether the flying gallop was the
correct posture of the horse in rapid motion. His publi-

cation 'The Horse in Motion' described the results of
his experiments. He did further research on the subject
for the University of Pennsylvania and published his
findings in 'Animal Locomotion' (1887). This monumental work contains 781 plates and is still the most
comprehensive work of its kind. The most valuable
photographs were those taken of a galloping race-
horse, for which he used a row of up to 36 small
cameras with clockwork shutters, and showed, for the
first time, how a horse lifts all four legs off the ground
when it is in fast motion.

An incredulous public rapidly perceived the absur-
dity of the 'rocking horse' attitude of horses' legs in
paintings throughout history. Muybridge's researches,
together with those of Marey in France and Eakins in
America, all of whom studied both human and animal
form in motion, threw an entirely new world at the

JOHN ATKINSON GRIMSHAW.
Boats at Whitby. Board. 8½ × 17½
inches. Signed and dated 1878.
Ferrers Gallery, London.

FRANK MEADOW SUTCLIFFE.
Whitby Harbour. Sutcliffe Gallery,
Whitby, Yorks.
Photograph taken c.1880–90.

HENRY PEACH ROBINSON. *Day's Work Done.* Royal Photographic Society of Great Britain.

Taken in 1877.

Opposite page, above:
DAVID ROBERTS, R.A. *Great Temple at Baalbek.* Panel. 30×42 inches. Mr John Goelet.

Roberts painted at least nine views of Baalbek between 1840 and 1861.

Opposite page, below:
View of Baalbek. Radio Times Hulton Picture Library, London.

Sepia photograph taken c. 1870-1880.

Below left:
EADWEARD MUYBRIDGE (1830-1904). *Galloping Horse.* Victoria and Albert Museum, London.

Taken in 1883-5. Muybridge's experiments, published in 'Animal locomotion' (1887), together with the experiments of E. J. Marey and J. D. B. Stillman revealed for the first time movement which could not be perceived by eye. Also revealed was the unreality of the 'rocking-horse' motion adopted by Sporting and Battle painters for centuries. W. G. Simpson wrote in 'The Magazine of Art' (1883): 'It is not a renaissance we are to expect, but a revolution; for it appears that, except now and again by accident artists from all time have wrongly represented the paces of Quadrupeds.'

Below right:
STANLEY BERKELEY. *For God and the King.*

From a detail of an etching after *For God and the King* by Stanley Berkeley exhibited at the Royal Academy in 1889.

painter's feet. One immediate result was that the Academies of the world were inundated with battle pictures, showing horses charging in every direction, with all four legs off the ground. Not since 1815 had the Battle of Waterloo been so popular! Another result of these movement photographs was more subtle: once it was found the new treatment of movement represented visual truth, the critics of hard-edge Pre-Raphaelitism found the static representation of nature less palatable than ever. Charles Kingsley, for instance, criticized the lack of movement in Pre-Raphaelite pictures for being 'unnatural'. What they tried to represent as still 'never yet was still for the thousandth

part of a second'. They strove 'to set a petrified Cyclops to paint his petrified brother'. ('Two Years Ago', 1857). Photography had already made panoramic paintings like *Derby Day* a possibility. Now movement, as recorded by the camera lens, had entered the artistic consciousness.

The uses of photography in printing entirely altered the character and direction of the pictorial arts allied to painting. Frith lamented in his memoirs that photography 'bids fair, in the modern shape of photogravure, to destroy line, and all other styles of engraving, as effectually as it has put a stop to lithography'. What Frith does not mention is that photography, in its auxiliary uses, popularised his pictures and those of his contemporaries to a hitherto unattainable degree, thereby enabling many a Victorian artist to lead a life of comfort, or even luxury, on the proceeds of mass distribution. Furthermore, the photographing of treasures throughout the world, the use of photographs in lectures (a practice Ruskin was not slow to adopt), and reproductions in books and periodicals, all led to a rapid dissemination of knowledge and the formation of taste. Photographs of archaeological sites, like Pompeii, and others of antiquities in Greek and Italian museums rapidly familiarized the public with the objects and background in paintings by the

neo-classicists, such as Leighton and Alma-Tadema, who themselves surely benefited from the study of photographs and reproductions to obtain archaeological accuracy. Alma-Tadema was, in fact, an active photographer: Birmingham University owns no less than a hundred and sixty-four volumes of his photographs of archaeological sites and classical antiquities. Whistler, who, after the discovery of Tanagra in the 'seventies, was strongly influenced by Hellenistic terracotta statuettes and other objects of classical antiquity, owned an album of photographs of such pieces. No other invention ever rendered painting such a service.

XIV

PORTRAITURE

> *'Painting is worthless, except portrait painting'*—Carlyle

The death of Sir Thomas Lawrence in 1830 marked the end of the great age of portrait painting in England. Had there been a painter of equivalent mastery who aspired to succeed him, it is doubtful whether, under the prevailing conditions, he could have stayed the course. The irruption of photography, changing social conditions, the popularity of genre painting, the long-awaited triumph of landscape painting for which Gainsborough had earlier hankered, and the prestige of High Art, all conspired to reduce the chances of the Victorian portrait painter. This is not to say that no portraits were being painted, merely that few painters, and these mostly of moderate talent, succeeded in making a living almost entirely out of portraiture.

Photography had emerged as a symbol of the forces of democracy. The procedure of having one's likeness committed to canvas was regarded as either an act of canonization, or as pleasing documentary evidence that one existed, or, better still, that one had attained, through breeding, money or both, a high level of civilized existence. Now, however, an accurate likeness could be obtained in a few minutes for sixpence or a shilling (Mayhew's 'photographic man' boasted that he took as many as a hundred and forty six photographic portraits in one day, 'and the majority was shilling ones'). So having a likeness recorded was no longer the preserve of the rich and the aristocratic. Moreover, the blandishments of High Art engendered contempt for portraiture. Barry, Haydon and the young Watts all regarded portraiture as a last resort, amounting to no more than a tiresome interruption in their pursuit of lofty idealism. When Lord Holland talked Watts into painting Lady Holland, Haydon could scarcely contain himself. Though Watts, he said, went to Italy 'for Art, for High Art, the first thing the

WILLIAM ETTY, R.A. *Mlle Rachel.* Millboard. 24 × 18 inches. City of York Art Gallery, York.

The identity of the sitter is based on a similarity with other known portraits. The sitter's real name was Eliza Félix (1821-1858), a great French tragedienne. The portrait was probably painted on her first visit to England in 1841.

LORD LEIGHTON OF STRETTON, P.R.A. *Sir Richard Burton.* 23½ × 19½ inches. National Portrait Gallery, London.

Exhibited at the Royal Academy in 1876. This portrait of Sir Richard Burton (1821-1890), the famous explorer, was painted in that year.

210

ALFRED STEVENS. *Mary Ann, Wife of Leonard Collmann.* 27¾ × 21¾ inches. Tate Gallery, London.

Leonard Collmann, an architect and interior decorator, was a friend of Stevens and a fellow student in Florence. The picture was painted in about 1854.

LORD LEIGHTON OF STRETTON, P.R.A. *Letty.* 19 × 16 inches. Stone Gallery, Newcastle-upon-Tyne.

Exhibited at the Royal Academy in 1884. This is a portrait of Lena Dene, the youngest of five sisters who had lost their parents. Four of the girls became favourite models with Leighton. Among the pictures for which Lena modelled were *Cymon and Iphigenia* (1884) and *Captive Andromache* (1888). The picture was much admired by Ruskin.

English do is to employ him on *Portrait*! Lord Holland I understand, has made him paint Lady Holland!! Is this not exquisite? Wherever they go, racing, cricket, trial by jury, fox-hunting, and portraits are the staple commodities first planted or thought of. Blessed be the name of John Bull!' When Haydon painted ninety-seven portraits in his vast *Reform Banquet*, Lord Jeffrey failed to identify a single person; and yet his ruminative portrait of Wordsworth is a *tour de force*, and evidence of the loss incurred through his sacrificing himself to High Art.

To most Victorian painters portraiture was little more than a side-line, and most of them practised it. In the early years these painters included Wilkie, Etty and Landseer. Frith, William Quiller Orchardson (1832–1910), James Sant (1820–1916), John Collier (1850–1934), James (Joseph-Jacques) Tissot (1836–1902), Hubert von Herkomer (1849–1914), Frank Holl (1845–1888) and Luke Fildes (1844–1927) were all subject painters who achieved, to a greater or lesser degree, distinction as portraitists. Of these, Holl and Fildes devoted themselves almost entirely to portraiture in their maturity. The Pre-Raphaelites and their associates contained some notable portrait-painters in their ranks, including Rossetti, Madox Brown, Sandys,

Burne-Jones, Holman Hunt and Millais. With the exception of Madox Brown and Millais, the Pre-Raphaelites were, as would have been expected, very subjective in portraiture, which was usually integrated with their distinctive creative vision. John Linnell was the only notable landscape painter who could turn out the occasional portrait of distinction. Of the neo-classical painters, Leighton, Poynter and Alma-Tadema made successful portraits. Alfred Stevens, whose versatility makes him difficult to classify, painted a handful of outstanding portraits. G. F. Watts, on the other hand, is still considered as the foremost Victorian portrait painter before the arrival of Sargent, although he regarded this genre as second in importance to his allegorical painting.

The effect of photography on portraiture has been

discussed in the previous chapter. It is worth considering here one more aspect of this effect, however, in some statistics culled by Mr David Piper. Out of a total of 1,278 exhibits at the Royal Academy exhibition of 1830, just over half were portraits, of which three hundred were miniatures or small water-colours, and about eighty-seven in sculpture. At the 1870 Academy, portraits accounted for a bare fifth of the exhibits, while the number of sculptures (fulfilling a three-dimensional function denied to photography) actually increased to one hundred and seventeen. And what were the portraits like? As Dickens's Miss La Creevy says, 'there are only two styles of portrait painting; the serious and the smirk'. Thanks to the searching camera lens, the 'serious' was gaining ground, but throughout the century there was a steady demand for the pretty full-length, which could hang alongside ancestral portraits by Reynolds, Gainsborough and Romney. One of the best and most typical of the painters who supplied these was Richard Buckner (exhib. 1842–1877), 'a most kind and honest man', who had advised Leighton on the despatch of *Cimabue* from Rome. Millais, whose portraits contain echoes of

SIR JOHN EVERETT MILLAIS, Bt., P.R.A. *Only a Lock of Hair.* Panel. 14⅜ × 10⅜ inches. City Art Galleries, Manchester. Painted in about 1859. The sitter was Helen Petrie.

FRANZ XAVER WINTER-HALTER. *Lady Middleton.* 94 × 58 inches. Signed and dated 1863. The Rt Hon. Lord Middleton. Julia Louisa Bosville married Henry, 9th Lord Middleton in 1843.

Velasquez, Titian and Van Dyck, clearly sought to rival Reynolds's *The Ladies Waldegrave*, which he had seen at Strawberry Hill, in his lovely *Hearts are Trumps*. While, on the face of it, Velasquez gradually became the example to Victorian portrait painters (Francis Grant admitted that much of his success was owed to the Spanish painter, and Frank Holl became known as 'the English Velasquez'), Van Dyck, Reynolds and Gainsborough were still clearly discernible influences. New fashions in clothing tend to obscure this lineage. While the emergence of the hooped skirt in the 'forties, followed by the flowering of the crinoline, was grist to satirical draughtsmen, like John Leech and George Cruikshank, it was generally played down by the portrait painters, who often portrayed their subjects seated. Only the court painters, like the international Franz Xaver Winterhalter (1806–1873), and to a lesser extent, George Hayter, managed to do full justice to the crinoline.

The vanity, availability, ubiquity or downright reluctance of famous people to sit for portraits, and the accidents of chance, all played an important role in the Victorian era, as in any other. Thomas Carlyle, in many ways the embodiment of his age, was both vain and ubiquitous. In spite of his expressed contempt for artists, he regarded portraits as important documents. Even so, Carlyle's rugged features were frequently subordinated to the dictates of the artists'

Left:
ALFRED STEVENS. *John Morris Moore.* 23½ × 18¾ inches. Tate Gallery, London.
Moore, a well-known connoisseur and 'Verax' of 'The Times' shared a studio in Rome with Stevens in 1840. This portrait probably dates from that year.

RICHARD BUCKNER. *Adeline, 7th Countess of Cardigan.* 48 × 30 inches. Signed. Edmund Brudenell, Esq.
Painted between 1858 and 1868.

SIR JOHN EVERETT MILLAIS, Bt., P.R.A. *Hearts are Trumps*. 65¼ × 86½ inches. Signed with monogram and dated 1872. Tate Gallery, London.

Exhibited at the Royal Academy in 1872. Portraits of Elizabeth, Diana and Mary, daughters of Walter Armstrong, playing at dummy whist. Their dresses were designed by Millais.

creative vision, whether as a means to evoking a mood as in Whistler's famous portrait, or as part of the intense search for fundamental reality as in the case of Watts's apparently wayward portrait. G. K. Chesterton quotes Carlyle's disgusted conclusion on seeing it, that Watts had made him look 'like a mad labourer'. On reflection, Chesterton himself concluded that 'Watts painted Carlyle "like a mad labourer" because Carlyle was a mad labourer.' Watts and Millais could both enjoy the certainty of an endless supply of illustrious sitters, but a more wilful personality like Whistler was a frequent victim of chance. Clash of temperament no doubt contributed to his failure to go beyond one sitting for his portrait of Sarah Bernhardt. A long cherished desire to paint Disraeli seemed on the verge of fulfilment when he chanced upon the great man seated alone in St. James's Park. In answer to Whistler's hesitant request for the honour of painting his portrait, Disraeli 'gazed at him with lack-lustre eyes and murmured "go away, go away, little man".' As Graham Robertson, who tells the story, wrote, 'Whistler went, and with him

the great Poseur's chance of immortality on canvas. He shortly afterwards graciously assented to sit to Millais, who produced nothing in particular – to everybody's entire satisfaction.' On the other hand, Millais's finest portrait, which was also the finest portrait of Ruskin, resulted from the fraught propinquity of the two men at Glenfinlas prior to the breakdown of Ruskin's marriage to Effie and her elopement with Millais. Effie herself was a frequent model in Millais's pictures and the subject of many of his best portraits. Similarly, the women in Rossetti's life were transfigured in the mysteries of his poetic vision.

When Queen Victoria came to the throne, a number of portrait-painters practised in the long shadow cast by Lawrence. None of them attained his eminence. They included Martin Archer Shee (1769–1850), who succeeded Lawrence as President of the Royal Academy in 1830, an office which he held until his death twenty years later; in addition to his painting and official duties, he managed to publish poems, two novels and a play. Thomas Phillips (1770–1845) who in the early years of the century had painted sitters like

Byron, Blake, Scott, Southey, Crabbe and Coleridge, had a cool attractive style. Henry Perronet Briggs (1791–1844), as Baron Briggs, was the first, it will be remembered, in Thackeray's hierarchical exercise. Briggs, who was rescued from historical painting by portraiture, is best seen in his delightful studies and sketches. Francis Grant (1803–1878) was a portraitist of considerable style, at his best in an equestrian context. Grant became President of the Royal Academy, succeeding Eastlake in 1866 after the offer had been declined by Maclise and Landseer, and much to the disgust of Queen Victoria, who

wrote that Grant 'boasts of *never* having been in Italy or studied the Old Masters'.

The most indefatigable portraitist of all was Henry William Pickersgill (1782–1875), who was exhibiting portraits from 1806, a year after the Battle of Trafalgar, until 1872, a year after the Franco-Prussian war; few of the eminent escaped his brush, and when Phillips died in 1845, Pickersgill almost cornered the market. His portraiture was rarely more than adequate: the portrait of Wordsworth, for instance, is dully inarticulate compared with Haydon's. James Sant's exhibiting years were only two less than Pickersgill's. His picture

JAMES SANT, R.A. *The 7th Earl of Cardigan relating the Story of the Cavalry Charge of Balaclava to the Prince Consort and the Royal Children at Windsor.* 72 × 96 inches. Edmund Brudenell, Esq.

Portraits of James Thomas, 7th Earl of Cardigan (1797-1868) relating the story of the Charge of the Light Brigade to the Prince Consort and the Royal children at Windsor, 1854.

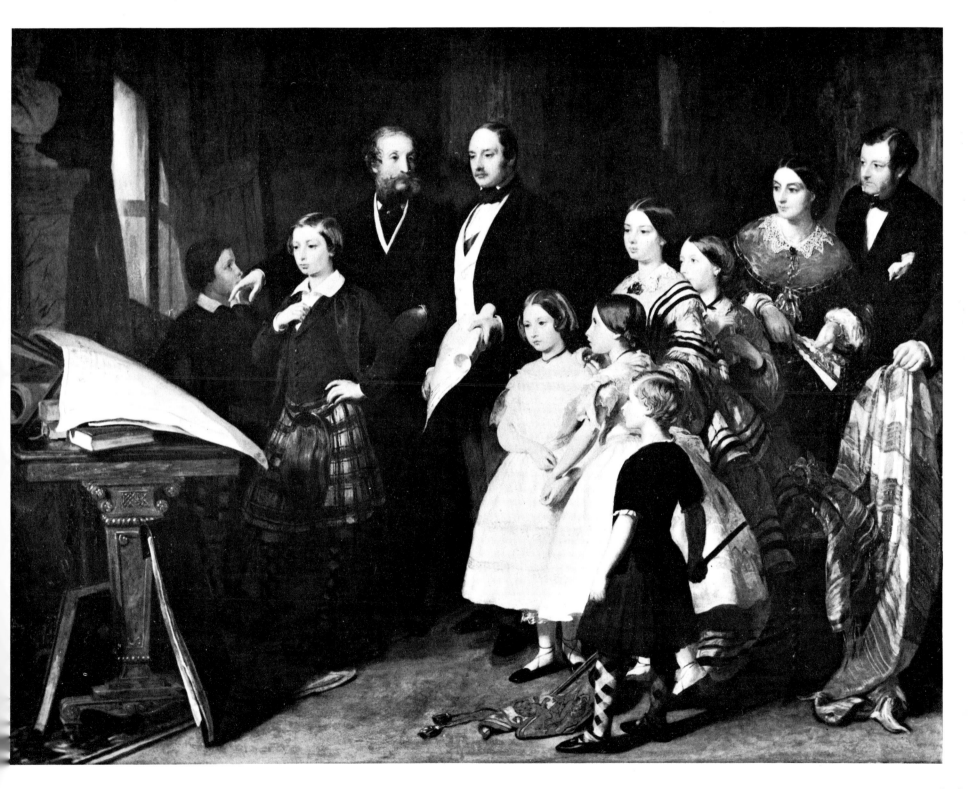

of *The 7th Earl of Cardigan relating the Story of the Cavalry
Charge of Balaclava to the Prince Consort and the Royal
Children at Windsor* is a typical Victorian group portrait.
He excelled, like Millais, in painting women. C. W.
Cope painted an interesting group portrait in *Selecting
Pictures for the Royal Academy*, which also provided a
glimpse inside this institution in the mid 'seventies.
Henry Tanworth Wells, the erstwhile miniaturist, who
turned to large scale portraiture in 1861, was a may-fly
by comparison with Sant, exhibiting for a mere fifty-
eight years. *Volunteers at the Firing Point*, though, reveals
a similar ability to paint a portrait group. His wife
Joanna Mary (1831–1861) was also a portraitist.
George Richmond (1809–1896), a member of a
dynastic painting family, and a friend of Blake, was a
distinguished artist whose ability to catch a likeness
was famous. His life-size chalk drawings of heads were
a formidable challenge to photography; he strained
after truth – 'Ah! but the truth lovingly told'. He only
began to paint in oils in 1846 and gave up regular

work in 1881, when he devoted some of his time to
sculpture. His sons, Thomas (1802–1874) and W. B.
Richmond were also very able portraitists. The
Scottish tradition of portraiture, stemming from
Raeburn, maintained by William Dyce in the
'thirties, persisted, though with a higher degree of
finish, through the work of John Watson-Gordon
(?1790–1864) to George Fiddes Watt (1873–1960).

The painters associated with the Pre-Raphaelite
movement were, on the whole, too preoccupied by the
literary content of their themes to spare time for
portraiture. This is something of a loss, since their
meticulous regard for detail and intensity of vision
were qualities which lent themselves to portrait
painting. However, their habit of using each other and
their friends as models resulted in a number of like-
nesses in their subject pictures, notably in the portraits
of the artist and his wife in Madox Brown's *The Last of
England* and the multiple portrait group in Millais's
Lorenzo and Isabella. According to W. M. Rossetti,

Elizabeth Siddal's best likenesss is in *Ophelia*. Holman Hunt's portraits were all too few. The head of the fanatical Canadian fruit-farmer, *Henry Wentworth Monk*, at the National Gallery of Canada, conveys with subtle insight his subject's fervour. The Pre-Raphaelite movement produced at least one outstanding portrait painter in Frederick Sandys, a constantly impecunious but elegant friend of Rossetti, who considered him 'the most brilliant of living draughts-men'. Esther Wood, who wrote a monograph on the artist during his life-time, saw in him a 'fearless portrayer of the more malignant aspects of woman-hood'. Although she was referring to the tragic subject pictures, such as *Medea* and *Morgan Le Fay*, his portraits of old ladies such as *Mrs Anderson Rose* and *Mrs Jane Lewis* and old gentlemen like *The Rev. James Bulwer*, show him as an artist of penetrating yet not unkindly perception. His crayon portraits with their naturalistic

facial features against mannered backgrounds, reminis-cent of Rossetti, are the best of their kind since the early work of George Richmond.

It is to Watts that we must turn for the strongest link between the vanishing glories of the school of Lawrence and the new era of portraiture heralded by Sargent in the 'eighties. Compelled by the necessity to earn a living on his return to England from Italy in mid-career, he reluctantly took to portraiture with the bashful disdain of a retired army major obliged to augment his pension by administering the accounts of a golf-club. His friends, Lord Holland and the Prinseps, promised to introduce him to the most eminent people of his time. Thus Watts was confronted with a seemingly endless succession of the greatest, noblest and most powerful of the Victorians, and he brought to his portraiture the same high-minded attitude which had

CHARLES WEST COPE, R.A. *The Council of the Royal Academy selecting Pictures for the Exhibition.* 57 × 86½ inches. Initialled and dated 1876. Royal Academy, London.

Exhibited at the Royal Academy in 1876. The group includes por-traits of the President, Sir Francis Grant, J. F. Lewis, Leighton, Millais and the artist himself.

guided his essays in allegorical painting. It is difficult to escape the same conclusion as that arrived at by Chesterton, that Watts was as allegorical in his portraits as he was in his allegories, that 'he is allegorical when he is painting an old alderman'. To Watts, a portrait

WILLIAM HOLMAN HUNT, O.M. *Henry Wentworth Monk.* 20 × 26 inches. Signed with monogram and dated 1858. National Gallery of Canada, Ottawa.

Exhibited at Liverpool in 1860. H. W. Monk (1827-1896) who was an early advocate of world peace and Zionism, was born and died in Canada. He met Holman Hunt in Palestine.

Below left:
ANTHONY FREDERICK AUGUSTUS SANDYS. *The Revd James Bulwer.* Panel. 29¾ × 21¾ inches. National Gallery of Canada, Ottawa.

Probably painted between 1861 and 1866. Bulwer (1794-1879) was a naturalist, antiquarian, and friend and pupil of John Sell Cotman.

Above right:
FORD MADOX BROWN. *Lucy Madox Brown.* Board. 6¼ inches diameter. Mrs Roderic O'Conor.

Lucy Madox Brown (1843-1894), herself to become a talented artist, was the artist's daughter by his first wife Elizabeth Bromley. This portrait probably dates from about 1848.

Below right:
SIR FRANCIS GRANT, P.R.A. *Mary Isabella Grant.* 50 × 40 inches. Leicester Museum and Art Gallery.

Exhibited at the Royal Academy in 1850. The sitter, who was the artist's daughter, died in 1854.

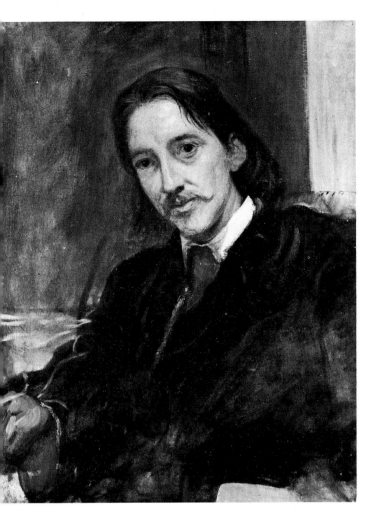

person, not the record of accidental position or arrangement of light and shadows.' No doubt this was a tilt at the way portraiture was going in the 'seventies. Whistler entitled two of his outright masterpieces, the portraits of his mother and of Carlyle, as *Arrangement in Grey and Black No 1* and *Arrangement in Grey and Black No 2*. Portraiture to Whistler was primarily a means to an induction of mood and the sitter was always carefully related to the background: it was an act of progressive refinement. Theodore Duret recalled that Whistler, with careful regard for colour and tone, brought his portrait nearly to completion, and then rubbed it out, starting all over again for as many as ten times. Like Sargent, Whistler brought to English portraiture the influence of Frans Hals, as well as the

was not merely a likeness, but an interpretation and a revelation, compounded of mind and soul, of the sitter's greatness: 'He scarcely ever paints a man,' wrote Chesterton, 'without making him five times as magnificent as he really looks. The real men appear, if they present themselves afterwards, like mean and unsympathetic sketches from the Watts original.' The portraits of his friend Tennyson appear to us as sombre evocations of grandeur, but withdrawn and detached, and existing on a plane beyond the comprehension of ordinary mortals. The portrait of Tennyson when he was about fifty-four, at the National Portrait Gallery, bears a striking but fortuitous resemblance to the face on the Turin Shroud. It has been said that Watts could not paint women, but this is hardly true of his early period which produced, for example, *Lady Holland*, painted in 1844, and the portrait of *Lady Margaret Beaumont and her Daughter*, in the collection of Viscount Allendale. In charming portraits such as these, and in *Lady Holland in a Chapeau de Paille* in the Royal collection, Watts could forget himself and revel in sumptuous textures and alluring colours. His portraits are more accessible to us as paintings than are his allegories, and yet they appear as formidable symbols of an age which is still, to many, one of irritating grandeur and complacency.

'A portrait,' said Watts, 'should have in it something of the monumental; it is a summary of the life of a

GEORGE FREDERICK WATTS,
O.M., R.A. *William Morris*.
25½ × 20½ inches. National Portrait
Gallery, London.

Painted in 1880. This portrait of
William Morris (1834-1896), soci-
alist, poet, artist and manufacturer,
is posed, appropriately, against a
background of wall-paper.

Opposite page, above left:
GEORGE FREDERICK WATTS,
O.M., R.A. *Lady Holland on a Day
Bed.* 14 × 18½ inches. Watts Gallery,
Compton.

This portrait of Mary Augusta,
Lady Holland (1812-1889) was pro-
bably painted at the Villa Roccella,
Naples where Watts stayed with the
Hollands in 1844-5.

Opposite page, below left:
JAMES McNEILL WHISTLER.
*Arrangement in Grey and Black, No 2:
Thomas Carlyle.* 67⅞ × 56½ inches.
Signed with Butterfly device. Glas-
gow City Art Gallery and Museum.

Exhibited at 48 Pall Mall, 'Mr
Whistler's Exhibition', 1874. This
portrait of Thomas Carlyle (1795-
1881), painted in 1872-3, was one
of Whistler's earliest on a large
scale. *Arrangement in Grey and Black,
No 1: The Artist's Mother* had been
exhibited at the Royal Academy in
1872. Whistler recorded that when
Carlyle was ready for the first sitting,
he said: 'And now, mon, fire away!'
Noticing Whistler's surprise, he
added: 'If ye're fighting battles or
painting pictures, the only thing to
do is to fire away!'

HERBERT JAMES DRAPER.
The Lament for Icarus. 72×61¼ inches. Tate Gallery, London.

Exhibited at the Royal Academy in 1898, and purchased under the terms of the Chantrey Bequest for £840.

Opposite page, below:
JOHN CALLCOTT HORSLEY, R.A. *A Pleasant Corner.* 30×22 inches. Royal Academy, London.

Exhibited at the Royal Academy in 1866. This was Horsley's Diploma Work; he had been elected R.A. in 1864.

life with grandiose ambitions, studying fresco painting in Munich and Italy and winning two prizes in the competition for decorating the Houses of Parliament.

His fresco perished along with his original ambitions and he devoted himself to painting scenes from rural and domestic life with sweetness and elegance.

Webster's relative, Frederick Daniel Hardy (1827–1911), painted mainly domestic interior scenes, as did George Bernard O'Neill (1828–1917), who survived for twenty years after the last occasion on which he exhibited a picture. Possibly the most interesting of this group is A. E. Mulready (exhib. 1863–1886). This artist, about whom little is known, was, to risk a contradiction in terms, a sentimental social realist. Like so many of the more intriguing minor Victorian artists, he was repetitive, but the numerous little pictures of waifs, strays and ragamuffins are a true commentary on late nineteenth century poverty which, notwithstanding Lord Shaftesbury's philanthropic reforms, was still part of the social scene.

The second and larger group, known as the 'St John's Wood Clique', was more diffuse, its most unifying bond being a fondness for practical jokes. Its leader, Philip Hermogenes Calderon (1833–1898), was the son of a truant Spanish priest who joined the Protestant Church and later became Professor of Spanish literature at King's College in London. Calderon's first successful picture, *Broken Vows*, is a sharp essay in Pre-Raphaelitism. William Frederick

JOHN WILLIAM NORTH. *Halsway Court, North Somerset.* Water-colour. $13 \times 17\frac{1}{2}$ inches. Inscribed 'N '65'. Robin de Beaumont, Esq.

The Victoria and Albert Museum have a pencil sketch for this water-colour. The figures in the pencil drawing were added by Pinwell.

Opposite page, above left:
GEORGE JOHN PINWELL. *The Strolling Players.* Water-colour. $17\frac{3}{4} \times 14\frac{1}{2}$ inches. Signed and dated '67. Robin de Beaumont, Esq.

The centre group is said to include portraits of Pinwell and his wife.

A London Crossing Sweeper and a Flower Girl by A. E. Mulready is reproduced in colour on p. 255.

Yeames (1835–1918) was born in Russia, the son of a British consul. His *And when did you last see your Father?* represents to many the consummation of the historical genre picture, its very title a subject of mirth.

The work of the black and white illustrators of the 'sixties in such periodicals as 'Punch', 'The Cornhill Magazine' and 'Once a Week' had a strong formative effect on later genre painting. 'The Graphic' founded in 1869 by W. L. Thomas was the most influential of all. Some artists including Luke Fildes (1844–1927) and Frederick Walker (1840–1875), often later worked up their illustrations into oil paintings. 'The Graphic' was deeply committed to social observation, and from this stemmed the brief period of social realism in the 'seventies. Charles Keene (1823–1891) was an incisive graphic commentator, who too rarely digressed into oils. The successive deaths in 1875 of Frederick Walker, Arthur Boyd Houghton (b. 1836) and George John Pinwell (b. 1842), at the age of thirty-five, thirty-nine and thirty-three respectively, were a sad loss for English painting. All three were artists of tantalizing promise. Even so, the work of Fred Walker

took a strong hold over the imagination of his contemporaries. He was described by Tom Taylor as a 'nervous, timid, sensitive young fellow, frail and small of body, and feverish of temperament'. Walker exhibited *The Lost Path* in 1863: although it was 'skied' at the Royal Academy and sold for a meagre sum, it was engraved six years later in 'The Graphic'. The pathetic figure of the woman carrying her child in the snow was reflected in Fildes's engraving, 'Houseless and Hungry', which he painted five years later under the title *Applicants for Admission to a Casual Ward*. Walker's friend Pinwell had a more volatile temperament, and his work is uneven; it seems that he never fully understood the chemical qualities of body-colour. 'Ah! my boys,' prophesied Arthur Boyd Houghton with rueful accuracy at Pinwell's funeral, 'you will be planting me here also before three months'. One of the ablest of the illustrators, he painted intermittently in oils throughout his short life. John William North (1842–1924) was more fortunate, surviving well into the present century. North influenced Walker, who occasionally drew the figures in North's pictures, as

Opposite page, right:
CHARLES KEENE. *In the Studio.* Millboard. $8\frac{3}{4} \times 6$ inches. Initialled. Villiers David, Esq.

The picture is inscribed on the reverse: 'J. P. Heseltine Esq with C. Keene's kind regards'. The girl, who was a Langham sketching Club model, is holding a sheet of music.

Opposite page, below left:
THOMAS WEBSTER, R.A. *The Frown.* $12\frac{1}{2} \times 25$ inches. Signed and dated 1842. Guildhall Art Gallery, London.

Replica to the picture which was exhibited at the Royal Academy in 1841, and companion to *The Smile.* Both pictures, which were accompanied by quotations from Goldsmith's 'Deserted Village', were very popular in their day.

FREDERICK WALKER, A.R.A.
The Lost Path. 36×28 inches.
Signed and dated 1863. The Rt
Hon. Lord Sherfield, G.C.B.,
G.C.M.G.

Exhibited at the Royal Academy
in 1863. This picture, for which
his sister, Mary, was the model, was
Walker's first important oil-painting.
Salt was used to convey an impression of snow on her dress. The
subject was first used by the artist
as an illustration to a poem,
'Love in Death' in 'Good Words'
(March 1862). He used photographs
as an aid, since, as he wrote in his
diary, he felt 'anxious to begin
carefully and from nature'.

also did Pinwell. George Heming Mason (1818–1872) was another talented painter whose untimely death in the early 'seventies was a further blow to English painting; older than any of the young illustrators, he began to gain recognition at the same time as they did. John Dawson Watson (1832–1892) exhibited a number of domestic and outdoor scenes; *Children At Play* shows the application of Pre-Raphaelite principles. Although he was not an illustrator, the work of John Lee (fl.1850–1860), a Liverpool artist, is a striking testimony to the triumph of Pre-Raphaelitism in the provinces.

Frank Holl, Hubert von Herkomer (1849–1914), and Luke Fildes, were all early contributors to 'The Graphic'; they wrought pathos from social realism,

translated the themes of their illustrations into oil-paint, and, when genre painting began to fall out of favour, they all took to portraiture. Holl's *Newgate: Committed for Trial* is a movingly expressive picture, full of compassion. Herkomer, who was born in Bavaria and died in Budleigh Salterton, became a famous Victorian figure, gathering money and honours. An early admirer of Fred Walker, he was also an original stage-designer, and lived to design sets for the cinema. Herkomer claimed to have learned in England that 'truth in art should be enhanced by sentiment'. He was rarely sentimental, but his social realism is rather heavy-handed and clogged with over-emphasis, as can be seen in *On Strike*. Fildes painted some of the finest later genre pictures. He used to search for

WILLIAM DYCE, R.A. *Pegwell Bay, Kent – a Recollection of October 5th*, 1858. 25×35 inches. Tate Gallery, London.

Exhibited at the Royal Academy in 1860, this picture represents a continuation of the tradition of scenes at the seaside. Frith's *Ramsgate Sands* had been exhibited in 1854. The figures in the foreground of Dyce's picture are, from the right, his wife, her two sisters and one of his sons. Donati's comet is in the sky. *See p. 227.*

Children at Play by J. D. Watson is reproduced in colour on p. 256.

237

works, defy classification. Samuel Baldwin (exhib. 1843–1858) combined a Ruskinian eye for landscape with figure painting in *Sketching Nature*. Sophie Anderson (1823–after 1898) is now remembered for the exquisite *No Walk To-day*. Charles West Cope (1811–1890) is best remembered for his charming scenes of mothers and children. Abraham Solomon (1824–1862), elder brother of the ill-fated Simeon, began by exhibiting pictures of the 'V–c–r of W–kef–ld' variety, and scored a great success in 1854 with the exhibition of two scenes from contemporary life, *First Class—The Meeting . . . and at first meeting loved* and *Second Class – The Parting*, both set in railway carriages with the popular themes of love and emigration. *The Travelling Companions*, painted in 1862 by Augustus Egg, and now at Birmingham, one of the loveliest of Victorian pictures, is also set in a railway carriage, and is distinguished by a complete absence of moralizing. Pre-Raphaelitism

FREDERICK SMALLFIELD. *First Love.* 30⅛ × 18⅛ inches. Signed and dated 1858. City Art Galleries, Manchester. The picture illustrates a ballad by Thomas Hood.

JOHN J. LEE. *Sweethearts and Wives*. 33¼ × 28 inches. Signed with monogram and dated 1860. Mr and Mrs Norman Parkinson.

The scene is Liverpool Docks. In the middle distance to the right is H.M.S. Majestic, a wooden screw ship of the line, which had done service in the Baltic during the Crimean War. At the time the picture was painted, she was on Coast Guard service. It has been suggested that Lee's models did duty for more than one head, and that the sailor on the right is a self-portrait. It seems probable that this was the picture exhibited both at the Liverpool Academy (no. 227) and at Suffolk Street (no. 443) in 1861.

characters in his nightly wanderings in the streets of London: the top-hatted central figure in *Applicants for Admission to a Casual Ward* was made to stand on sheets of brown paper sprinkled with Keating's Powder, a pint mug of porter at his side. *The Doctor*, a wholly unsentimental study of medical compassion, enjoyed immense popularity, especially in America. Eyre Crowe (1824–1910), who in 1852 accompanied his cousin Thackeray on his lecture tour of America, was another painter with a penchant (only too rarely indulged) for social comment. A pupil of Delaroche and a friend of Gérôme, he was, however, naturally addicted to themes from history, and these comprised the greater part of his work.

Other painters of anecdotal subjects, some of them remembered for a handful of works or even for single

figures in the treatment of another public transport subject, *Omnibus Life in London*, painted three years earlier by William Maw Egley (1826–1916). George William Joy treated a similar metropolitan subject in *The Bayswater Omnibus*, thirty-six years later. Frank Stone (1800–1859) and his son Marcus (1840–1921) both reflected the styles of their successive generations: Frank in his sharpness of outline and bold colouring, and Marcus in his fondness for foppish quasi-Regency subject matter and looser treatment. Alfred Elmore (1815–1881) seems like a ghost from the past; born while the Battle of Waterloo was in progress, he ran the full gamut from historical painting to full-blooded

PHILLIPS, Olga Somech. *Solomon J. Solomon: A Memoir of Peace and War.* (n.d.).

(Ricketts, Charles R.A.). Self-Portrait taken from the Letters and Journals of Charles Ricketts, R.A.; collected and compiled by T. Sturge Moore, edited by Cecil Lewis (1939).

ROBERTSON, W. Graham. *Time Was* (1931).

ROTHENSTEIN, Sir John. *The Life and Death of Conder* (1938).

ROTHENSTEIN, William. *Men and Memories: recollections;* 2 vols. (1931-2).

R.P. *Sir William Orpen* (1923).

SCHMUTZLER, Robert. *Art Nouveau* (1964).

SICKERT, W. R. *Bastien Lepage: Modern Realism in Painting* (1892).

SINCLAIR, Archdeacon. *Joseph Farquharson, R.A.* (1912).

SINCLAIR, W. M. *John Macwhirter, His Life and Work* (1903).

SKETCHLEY, R. E. D. *J. W. Waterhouse, R.A.* (1909).

SPEAIGHT, Robert. *William Rothenstein: the Portrait of an Artist in his Time* (1962).

(Steer, P. Wilson). Catalogue of an exhibition given by the Arts Council; with an introduction by Andrew Forge (1960).

STIRLING, A. M. W. *The Richmond Papers* (1926).

STOREY, G. A. *Sketches from Memory* (1899).

SUTTON, Denys. *James McNeill Whistler* (1966).

THOMSON, D. Croal. *Sir Luke Fildes, R.A.* (1895).

(Tissot, James [Jacques-Joseph]). Catalogue of a retrospective exhibition given at the Museum of Art, Rhode Island School of Design, Providence, and The Art Gallery of Ontario, Toronto; with an introductory essay by Henri Zermer (1968).

(Tissot, James). Catalogue of an exhibition at the Barbican Art Gallery, ed. by Krystyna Matyjaszkiewicz (1984).

USHERWOOD, Paul and SPENCER-SMITH, Jenny. *Lady Butler, Battle Artist* (1987).

(Waterford, Louisa Marchioness of). Catalogue of a centenary exhibition at Lady Waterford Hall, Ford, Northumberland; with a foreword by Christopher Wood (1983).

(Waterford, Louisa Marchioness of). Catalogue of an exhibition of Water-colour Paintings, with a short memoir, at 8 Carlton Terrace (April 1910).

(Waterhouse, John William R.A.). Catalogue of an exhibition at the Mappin Art Gallery, Sheffield and Central Art Gallery, Wolverhampton; with an introduction by A. Hobson (1978-9).

WHISTLER, James McNeill. *'Ten o'clock'* lecture delivered 1885 (1888).

(Whistler, James McNeill). Catalogue of an exhibition jointly given by the Arts Council and Knoedler Galleries. New York; with an introduction by Andrew MacClaren Young (1960).

WILLIAMSON, George Charles. *Charles J. Pinwell and his Works* (1900).

INDEX